Opening to Life

Opening to Life

Reconnecting With Your Internal Source
of Energy, Wisdom and Joy

Kimberly Kingsley

Copyright © 2003, 2017 Kimberly Kingsley

All rights reserved. No part of this publication may be reproduced, distributed, or transmitted in any form or by any means, including photocopying, recording, or other electronic or mechanical methods, without the prior written permission of the publisher, except in the case of brief quotations embodied in critical reviews and certain other noncommercial uses permitted by copyright law.

TABLE OF CONTENTS

INTRODUCTION	xi
PERSONAL ALIGNMENT	1
The Treadmill Effect	3
Reversing the Flow	7
Exploring the Nature of Spirit	16
Timelessness	20
Abundance	25
Unified	27
Intelligence	29
Aligning Your Mind with the Nature of Life	37
Minimal Planning	38
Time to Be Still	39
Minimal Thinking	41
Abundance vs. Competition	43
Body Alignment	46
Exercise	53
RESTORING YOUR CONTAINER	57
Clearing Emotional Blocks	59
Emotions: Is it better to implode or explode?	74
Container Repair: Sealing Energy Leaks	82
Addictions	83

Karma	87
Beyond Back and Forth	91
Relationship Dynamics	**95**
Emotional Management	**101**
Conflict	**110**
Relationship Integrity	**113**
Power Struggles	118
Being Connected	124
Communication	126
Congruence	126
Good Boy, Good Girl	**134**
Directness	136
Concise	138
Listening	140

A HIGHER LIFE — 145

Redirecting Energy in Everyday Life	**147**
Money	148
Time	150
Work	154
Intuitive Knowing	156
Energy Refinement	159
Death	163
Ascension	**167**

Dedicated to Anna

The Brightest Star in My Universe

ACKNOWLEDGEMENTS

There are many people to thank for helping me complete this book. However, I must first acknowledge the unseen world of spirit, life, and love as my biggest recipient of gratitude. My next wave of thanks goes out to the people that have supported me in becoming the person I am today. My mother and father have forever provided me with unconditional love, support, and encouragement to do what I need to do in life. This gift has allowed me the freedom to take the risks necessary to attain my present level of humanness.

Thank you to all the people who provided encouragement throughout the process of writing this book. A great big thank you to Jan Allegretti, Kristine Kingsley, Jimmy Peggie, Shirley Hathaway, Hal Zina Bennett, and John Ruskan for your feedback and editing contributions to this book. Thank you to Michael Herzog for your design work on the first edition and to Brandon Tigrett for the second edition cover photo. I would also like to express deep appreciation to Kevin and Michelle O'Neill and Ron and Amy Kingsley for your unwavering support. Thank you Victoria and Dale Norris for the computer used for my first version! To Heather Cornwell: You are an angel who clearly had an assignment to help me learn how to see!

And finally, I would like to give a heartfelt "Thank You" to all my clients and people who have been in my classes and workshops: you have helped my heart grow by sharing your lessons on love, pain, and healing.

INTRODUCTION

IN THE YEARS PRIOR TO my learning about different qualities of energy, I appeared to the world to be like what most of us picture when we think of a twenty-something woman. I was working hard, spending lots of money, and generally appeared to have a fun-filled life. My life, however, was not the polished picture that others were seeing. While it's true that I was driving a nice car, had nice clothes, and a good job, my inner world painted a different picture. I felt anxious. I knew only that the pain of living was immense. It was almost as if I was drowning, but I couldn't figure out what I was drowning in.

One evening during this period of intense confusion I decided to go somewhere different for my daily run. Rather than go to the nearby canal, as I usually did, I went to the local university and ran around the track a couple of times. Running was one of the few things that brought me sanity, because it could quiet my obsessive thoughts. As I walked back to my car after my run, I spontaneously decided to climb up the hill that sits adjacent to the parking lot. As I stood at the top of this rocky hill and looked into the sky, a voice spoke to me. It said, "You have to go work on yourself so you can love others more." I realized immediately that this was an answer to a question I had been struggling with for sometime: my cousin had recently moved to Chicago and was looking for a suitable apartment, and I was thinking about joining her.

That voice would become very familiar over the next year. I eventually came to understand that it was my own voice, the voice that lives in the part of me that is connected to all of life. But from the moment I heard that first message, I knew that it spoke the truth. The following months were filled with packing my things and moving. Leaving the city where I grew up with my family and friends and many layers of external security looked a bit irrational. Nevertheless, I was filled with conviction that I was doing the right thing.

Within a month of arriving in Chicago I made two discoveries that would change my life forever. First, I saw a television program with an East Indian man who spoke about different body types, and foods that balance each type. The picture was fuzzy and the man's accent was thick, but I could not tear myself away from what he was saying. I learned later that the man on the TV was Deepak Chopra.

Later that week I read a newspaper that featured an article on Marianne Williamson's then new book, *A Return to Love*. The review contained several excerpts from the book. Though I was not actively searching for anything except my sanity, what I read made more sense than anything I had ever heard. I had often studied different religions and philosophies, but except for some early warm feelings for Jesus and an ongoing fondness for the principles of Buddhism, I did not have a spiritual path. Looking back, I realize the profound synchronicity of these two discoveries: during that time (and to this day) I did not watch television or read newspapers!

I went to the local bookstore, where I ended up spending an enormous amount of time, and purchased both of the books I had heard about. This started a reading frenzy that still has not ended, though its purpose has certainly changed. In addition, I began to take frequent walks to Lake Michigan, which was only a block away from my apartment. The lake was a valuable source of inspiration to me and to this day I consider it to be a sacred place.

I spent the next year crying tears of joy and sadness as I began to see that the way I had previously looked at life was only a partial glimpse at best. Gradually my vision had expanded to include the eternal dimension as well. It became clear that the dimension of spirit, life, or energy was more real than the physical life that I had been trying so desperately to make sense of. The deeper dimension emerged with a different set of laws, rules and values. Although I didn't realize it at the time, in the years that followed my life would literally turn upside down as my whole being reorganized itself to live according to this deeper truth.

Throughout that first year in Chicago I encountered one new revelation after another. My days were filled with long walks on the boardwalk of Lake Michigan, writing about my new thoughts, and reading every book that I could get my hands on that related to spirituality and healing. One cold day when I was sitting on the edge of the lake absorbing the beautiful surroundings, the following poem came to me from the same voice that had urged me to move to Chicago.

> I am a princess, special and frail,
> Basking in sunshine, a sunflower so pale.
> The lake is my spirit, wild and free.
> The sky is my limit, never ending pulling me.
> The sun is my energy, I am soaking it in
> So spirit can reign, again and again.
> The wind, it is love, pure and intense,
> Reflects off my body, finds others to touch,
> The people are my purpose, recipients of all above,
> The reason that I live, to give and get love.

That period of intense revelation and learning was the beginning of my life as I know it today, and it was also to be the end of life as I had formerly lived it. But the months and years following my initial awakening were not as effortless as I first assumed they would be. I soon discovered that the description of myself as a "princess" in the poem was an accurate depiction of my ego, and the part of me that was "special and frail" needed to be released so that I could access a deeper source of genuine strength. Although parts of this process were painful, it has been the most rewarding and transformative experience of my life. My new understanding did not change my life immediately, but it provided a very strong lifeboat to carry me through the period of integration that would follow.

My year in Chicago ended the same way it began. I started to ask myself if I should move back home. One Saturday morning as I sat by the lake I became very still, and that familiar voice spoke to me again. "You are on your path now," it said. "You might as well go be with the people who love you."

It was this experience that propelled me into the world of teaching and healing. Knowing that my life's purpose had been revealed, I went on to obtain the education and credentials of Professional Counselor. Teaching these laws of life gives me joy, because the life that flows through us is the ultimate source of joy.

More and more, people are making a place in their busy lives for spirituality through meditation, contemplation or reading about spiritual principles. *Opening to Life* is about taking this spiritual corner of life and bringing it together with the worldly part of life to create an existence that is both immensely powerful and spiritual at the same time. It is about bringing a quality of life into every moment of every day in our home, at work, with family, friends, and lovers. It is about finding heaven right here in the midst of everyday life rather than "out there" where our minds have put it. Many of us have taken the notion of God in heaven and generalized it to a heaven that is just out of reach all of the time. We have been conditioned to believe that heaven is just around the corner and within reach, but only *after* we obtain that dream job, *after* we retire, *after* we die…. In our constant yet elusive search for heaven, we often neglect a big part of heaven's home, the body. We reject it as a holy vessel and define it solely as a means for sensory pleasure. And while we neglect the true function of our bodies, we also neglect the sacred earth and all other parts of our matter or material selves that are mythically perceived as "dark." The irony of it all is that the only way to experience heaven is to embrace all of life, the dense world of flesh and earth as well as the airy freedom of the skies. In the process of reclaiming the parts of ourselves that we have denied, we emerge whole.

We have attempted to take a short cut in the pursuit of spirit. We have the unconscious belief that our spirit can be consumed, harnessed, or attained so we spend our days working, working, working, followed by eating and drinking and then some more work, in pursuit of what we think we have lost. The irony is that the void many of us are currently feeling will never be filled from these pursuits. It is time to slow down, turn around, and have a "prodigal son moment," celebrating that our true source of joy is not lost, but buried beneath a layer of emotional and physical debris.

This book is about making the shift inward toward your essential self, where life itself is quietly waiting to animate your days with energy, health and joy. This process is at once practical and profound, combining psychological techniques, physical balance, and spiritual principles to lead us into a way of life that has not existed for a very long time, if ever.

Introduction

Many of us have been trying to straddle two worlds simultaneously, being a spiritual person and then going out into the "real world" to make a living or socialize with friends. It is time to simplify and enrich our daily lives by allowing the vibrancy of spirit to penetrate our bodies, the places we work, and our homes.

Spirit does not live somewhere "out there" to be tapped into now and again. Spiritual energy is the very core of our being, and it is up to you to allow it to flow into your daily life and the environment that surrounds you. It is my hope that the message in this book tilts your world a little (or a lot) to make room for more life, love, peace, and yes, joy.

PERSONAL ALIGNMENT

The Treadmill Effect

ENERGY IS A COMMODITY LIKE money or grain. It is limited and finite in nature. All of us could do with more energy to get us through the day. Right? Not exactly.

The energy that most of us rely on to get up in the morning, eat breakfast, take our kids to school and attend twelve appointments in a row is limited, and hardly enough to allow us to feel sustained and refreshed throughout the day. We usually get ourselves going with coffee, some food, interaction with other people, and use the momentum of running on a treadmill day after day at 120 miles per hour to keep us moving along. This is the type of energy that most people are counting on when they think, "If I could just get to bed at a decent hour tonight, I would wake up rested." It's the short bursts of energy that we get from things like caffeine, calories and adrenaline that we want. But this way of thinking about energy is inaccurate and incomplete, as evidenced by the feeling of exhaustion we experience much of the time.

There is another source of energy that most everyone experiences from time to time, although they may have trouble figuring out how to tap into it as a primary source of fuel. This fresh, balanced, insightful, buoyant energy comes from a source deep inside each of us. We each have a direct connection to the source of all life. This source *is* life. Life, as I see it, is synonymous with spirit, energy, and our essential or deeper self. Spiritual life energy is the purest source of fuel, and it is obtained from the center of our being. Spirit is the universal property that animates all life forms. Soul is the eternal part of each of us that carries the blueprint of our being. Spirit without soul is formless and soul without spirit is dormant, thirsty or sleepy. Together they create the dance of life. Our internal connection to life is meant to feed and nourish us naturally at every level, starting with the soul, then expressing through our personality, mind and body. In order to receive this pure and potent energy we must actively cultivate the connection. Because this connection is often blocked or obscured we tend to look for artificial sources of energy to in the world around us. In this search, we are seeking fulfillment. There is only one problem: becoming *full* and *filled* from external energy sources is impossible. Why does one settle for artificial energy from the environment when the real thing is available from our own inner resources?

There are several reasons for this confusion. Simply put, we have been trained to seek energy and fulfillment by looking in the wrong direction–to the outside world rather than within. Social, professional, material and other outward avenues have become our primary source of fuel. These outward sources are distracting us from our true source of life-filled energy, which can sustain us at a much deeper level. In addition, we have learned along the way to turn away from the parts of ourselves that are hurting and in need of attention, so that we, in effect, reject the wounded parts of ourselves. As a result, an unproductive cycle occurs in which we shut down the flow of energy–both painful and joyful energy–from within, in exchange for a different kind of energy that somehow we have decided is safer and more valuable.

The body holds our unresolved trauma in the form of blocked emotions. Rejecting these emotions is a way of avoiding the unpleasant but necessary feeling of pain. Avoiding pain does not eliminate it because buried emotions always resurface somewhere. One of the ways that we avoid our emotional energy is through a highly developed defense mechanism called projection, in which we place unresolved trauma onto the outside world and then deny that it belongs to us. These unresolved emotions that we project outward carry an immense amount of energy with them. The energy carried in these projections is lost, and this ultimately causes us to seek replacement energy from outside ourselves. So rather than pulling the projections back, looking at our pain, and reclaiming our own energy, we seek to capture it from the external objects that are carrying our projections. For example, a person who has low self-esteem may place immense value on money and may "chase" money obsessively as a way to make him feel good about himself. In doing so, he has projected his value onto an outside object and is now attempting to capture it. Some other likely targets for our projections are other people, food, alcohol, work and just about anything else you can think of. The subject of projections will be discussed at length in the second section of the book.

Whatever method is used to avoid rather than deal with our painful emotions, the part of ourselves that we deny carries an immense amount of trapped energy. Because we are not aware of how to reclaim that energy, it is lost to us. This leads to the mistaken belief that we are starving. And in a starving frenzy we search for an alternative to what cannot be replaced: our own spirit. The soul, which is the primary vessel for spirit, is dormant from being ignored for so long. At this point we unconsciously run toward alternative energy sources such as work, food, shopping, alcohol, and each other, only to find that after consuming all that we can possibly handle, we are still starving.

Reversing the Flow

MAKING THE TRANSITION FROM AN external to an internal energy source entails **reversing the flow** of energy through the body. The process of making this transition is similar to reversing the direction of a moving object that already has a great deal of momentum. However, once the shift is made to living from the inside out, it is as natural as honey is to bees. Initially it takes effort to slow the momentum, and reconnect to oneself, though every step taken in that direction is massively reinforced with feelings of deep peace and contentment. These positive feelings help us to continue the initial work of reversing the flow.

If living from the inside out is so natural, why do most people rely on the limited energy that can be sucked out of the world? The reason is because there is a split within the psyche—both individually and collectively—that has occurred in part to avoid looking at our own pain, and in part due to the tendency to perceive spiritual values as separate from our daily lives. The split is between mind and body, between spirit and flesh. Therefore, the process of reversing the flow also involves mending that split by bringing the unconscious (rejected) part of oneself into consciousness.

This way of life has come to be part of our definition of the world. The addictive nature of society today is, in part, a result of people displacing their inherent value on the objects outside of themselves–and then chasing these objects in pursuit of Heaven or their own spirit. This phenomenon has gone so far that if we continue to stay on the present course we are in danger of destroying ourselves in the frantic search for self. With so much of our value placed on appearances, we, as a society, have forgotten who we fundamentally are.

This mode of existence has to be reversed because we are crashing and burning, as individuals, as families, as corporations, and as countries. We are running on the treadmill so fast that we have taught ourselves that we are here to run. The faster we run the better, the longer we run the better. Any problems keeping up the pace, just buy a new day timer; if you feel spread too thin, just hire a nanny; if you're on the road all the time, just get a cell phone.... On and on until YOU don't exist anymore. Or at least your soul doesn't–or it has become so small that it is imperceptible to you or to anyone else.

It is a huge risk for us to turn inward after chasing our own projections for so long. It entails slowing down, reassessing priorities, making changes and, most importantly, being able to realize that much of what we think of as "reality" is really our inner self projected onto the outer world. It's risky because we now believe that we are defined by how fast our lives travel. And finally it is a risk because reversing the momentum causes us to feel empty during the unfamiliar process of winding down and momentarily stopping the flow of energy long enough to ignite our internal source of energy. This can become so uncomfortable and alien that we would rather run to the nearest mall for a shopping spree than be still long enough to find ourselves again. After moving so fast for so long, feelings of lethargy alternating with terror may accompany this adventure into the unknown.

Choosing internal life energy can be frightening, and may cause even the most disciplined person to hop back on that daily treadmill just to reassure herself of who is in control. Choosing life energy in favor of external energy sources means giving up control, simply because life has a will of its own. But surrender to this greater will brings a life beyond our wildest dreams. Still, both the unknown and the fear of losing control often keep us tied to a predictable and mediocre existence. This existence lacks zest because it is fueled mostly from the lifeless energy we consume from the world around us.

The good news is that the willingness to experience the feelings of uncertainty and fear that so often come with change can lead us into a deeper, intensely more gratifying and fulfilling life. You see, by depending on the limited energy of the world without any knowledge of the reserves housed in the body, we have literally been blocking life. It has been suffocated and squeezed out resulting in a twisted form of expression. Fighting against ourselves, we begin to lose sight of the abundant life that lives within us. We then seek to devour external energy in place of expressing life energy through the unique vessel of our body and soul.

The fear that continually reappears when we begin to embrace the desire to shift our dependence from the superficial energy of the world to the deep energy of our essence is no less than the fear of annihilation. This is a very real feeling that needs to be acknowledged before we can make the gradual transition to wholeness. The fear of being consumed and annihilated comes from the part of us defined by the external world of forms–the personality, fighting to continue to be the ruler of our individual kingdom. A death does of sorts does occur when life is allowed to express itself as it was intended. At least it feels that way. This mini-death is similar to the death of a habit, only rather than quitting smoking, one is quitting the game of energy manipulation in favor of energy expression. This process of relinquishing external energy is an act of faith. You have to take the risk of turning away from feeding yourself drop by drop to go within where a river is waiting to provide an unending stream of nourishment. Turning away from the drops that have been your source of sustenance is an act of faith because the river isn't seen and felt until you turn away from the drops. Any act of faith involves going into uncharted territory. Instinct becomes the guide to lead you toward yourself, and instinct lives in the body rather than the mind. Attention shifts from the mind to the body and decisions are moved from the level of thinking to the level of intuitive feeling. Intuitive decisions coming from the body, where the soul lives,

Personal Alignment

support life instinctively, allowing life's energy to penetrate and radiate through all the levels of our being.

Does your energy come from deep within yourself or from the environment? The answer to this lies in the quality of energy that you experience. I use my internal state as a compass. On the days I feel strung out and distracted, nothing can satisfy me. I can easily make social plans, go buy something, have a big meal, and at the end of the day I am still restless. On the other hand–mostly when I make sure to take enough quiet time in the morning–there are days when I experience total inner peace. I feel content, open, receptive, and expressive at the same time. In this state, eating one grape is completely satisfying; being alone feels sacred and being with people feels like a blessing. Sometimes it is easier to blame our irritability on a "bad day" or a grumpy spouse than it is to take responsibility for how we perceive the world and others. However, freedom lies in knowing that the outer world reflects the inner world. This principle will be explored more in the section on projection. Just be mindful that if it seems that people are annoying, stop, turn around, and BE STILL. They will transform right before your eyes.

If you feel consistently buoyant, focused, content and productive, you are in touch with your inner self and are allowing the Energy of Life to fuel and lead you. If you feel distracted, strung out, and negative, punctuated by moments of energy after drinking a cup of strong coffee or receiving a good raise, then you are simply playing the energy exchange game.

Each of us is a vessel for the expression of spirit or life energy. This life energy moves through your soul, your mind, and your body, which are not necessarily distinct and separate. For example, more and more research is being done on the mind/body connection. The intricacies of how our being (spirit, soul, mind, body, and personality) intertwines and overlaps is not as relevant for the purpose of this book as is the concept that there are levels to our being. The first level is our spirit or our essence. This essence is what brings the other levels to life, animating our soul, mind, and body. The personality is a combination of all levels of our being (temperament), along with particular defense mechanisms and patterns of expression that we develop over time (ego). Our own container makes us unique, whereas the spirit we express makes us the same. Our function then, is to glorify the universal spiritual life through our own uniqueness. Simply put, when we are not fulfilling our function, we are not at peace. When we place appearances (body) over substance (spirit) we are confused and unhappy, because this perception reverses our function. When appearances are placed first we trick ourselves into thinking that our job is to preserve and defend our territory, which results in competition and hate, literally blocking the flow of life. When life energy is blocked we feel stagnant and go into consumption mode. Eating, drinking, spending–anything to get some energy. Herein lies the treadmill: as soon as we stop consuming we feel stagnant again and have to jump back on to get another jolt.

Life will lead if we let it. Letting life lead entails putting it in charge. Moving out of the way for something far more glorious than the most perfect body, house or car. It involves adopting an expressive orientation and to do this, you must open to life. The irony is that when you shift your goal to expressing life instead of chasing it, your body, home and world becomes beautiful. What's more lovely than a person who emanates love and vibrates with life? Life animates the body and the body grounds life. Without the body, life energy is unseen, but through us it is expressed in laughter, paintings, science or whatever we choose to create. Expressing ourselves simply means that our inner world feels open and still. Therefore, even if we are not talking or doing something we can be in an expressive state. Expressive and receptive are two sides of the same coin. Often you will be still and receptive, while other times you will choose to express the life that you receive. This is a simultaneous process, which occurs when we remember that our function is as a container.

Maintaining an expressive orientation rather than a consumptive orientation is the key. In an expressive orientation we are receptive to the life flowing through us, and it flows through us regardless of the presence or absence of activity. Being receptive to our internal source of energy is ALL we need to do. The rest happens naturally. Life takes over and moves our attention in the direction it needs to go. Just as a sunflower moves its face toward the sun, we place our attention on our inner spirit and we blossom. Life knows the direction it needs to go to flourish, though it is often ignored. Our task is to step back, relax into ourselves, and allow our lives to unfold before our very eyes.

So here we are, in need of a paradigm shift toward viewing our physical self as containers for true self-expression, rather than as objects to be adored or despised, depending on one's self-image. When we forget that we are more than our bodies, jobs, and possessions, we go into an existential crisis–"What is the meaning of life?" is the motto for this state of forgetfulness. More attention is paid to the sleek suit a person is wearing than to the twinkle in their eye. This has caused an identity crisis in the collective consciousness of humanity. We are lost. The more our attention is directed at the outer self, the more lost we become. We may expect that the attention that we place on outward pursuits (at the expense of our inner world) will come back as nourishment, but instead it returns in the form of addiction and compulsion in a desperate attempt to regain our energy. The difference is that when we are led from the deeper level, where spirit and soul live, we express energy, but when the personality or ego is leading, it simply exchanges energy with the environment. This energy exchange game easily fools us into thinking that we are making progress, expressing ourselves or being productive. In reality we are just spinning our wheels. The reason this state of being is not recognized as being unproductive, or even counter-productive, is that the personality is brilliant at defending against the truth and justifying its position.

The rest of this book is focused on how to ignite our soul with spirit and then allow that deepest part of our self (inner self) to direct and steer the rest of our being. I refer to this process as personal alignment. Personal alignment is essentially realigning oneself with spiritual energy rather than with material or addictive energy.

This process does not occur without difficulty. We have become frantic, addicted to seeking energy and fulfillment where it doesn't exist. It is inevitable that releasing that addiction is going to cause us to stumble and possibly fall, before we regain a sense of balance.

As we react to this deep feeling of existential crisis, we may look for a magic potion that will make us feel worthy and secure. That magic potion does not exist in events such as buying a new car or moving to another city, but it is fully present in the next breath you take. We must start to see that the animating power of the world lives within us, not in the outer world. By embracing this truth, we can surrender to the process of inner transformation. This allows the mysterious power of life to enter our bodies. We become safe in the knowledge that being shaken for a moment is a small price to pay for the gifts that an inspired life brings. Reversing the flow takes awareness, patience, and a little time–the result, however, is nothing less than enchanting.

Exploring the Nature of Spirit

RECENTLY A YOUNG WOMAN NAMED TONI came to me for counseling. She had worked hard to gain self-awareness on her own, and had even talked to another therapist a couple of times. Toni is a twenty-something woman who is about five feet nine inches tall and has long blond hair. She emanates pure radiance and health. Toni explained that, as a personal trainer, being in shape is a priority. "My problem is that I am obsessed with looking perfect, and it is making my life miserable," she told me.

As a recovering neurotic I could identify with Toni's struggles. When I asked about her spiritual beliefs, Toni said she was agnostic. I shared with her that I believed her over-identification with bodily perfection was a spiritual crisis.

Toni said, "At this point I am open to hearing anything."

After some discussion, Toni confessed that she had recently been feeling that perhaps God is present in nature. This disclosure was all it took to get Toni on the right track. We talked about spirit as being synonymous with life–the animating force of all life–and the ESSENCE OF WHO WE ARE. Toni seized on this concept just as enthusiastically as a football player grasps the ball while running to make a touch down. We spent some time discussing the nature of spirit, and Toni was on the path to inner peace.

The first step in the process of personal alignment is to reassign leadership to the deepest part of our Self, and thereby become aware of how spirit lives in and through us. Many of us have awakened to our spiritual side and are beginning to nurture that part of ourselves. The relationship we build with our essential nature will be the foundation for all future change and growth. This is the basis of personal alignment in that we put our deepest self in charge of our lives. Just as a car without a driver is without purpose and direction, without our ignited soul, we are simply wandering aimlessly through this world. Connecting with this very real part of ourselves is what gives our lives meaning. A life based on spirit becomes a purposeful expression of love, grounded in a sense of conviction found nowhere but here.

Personal alignment involves reordering values so that thoughts and actions line up with the nature of our inner self, rather than with material values. The soul and essential spirit live in an eternal realm that thrives under a set of principles that are entirely different from those of the material world. When we are not aware of the principles and laws under which our eternal self is able to thrive, we are cut off from life itself and from the nourishment and direction that it provides.

Most of us were trained–and continue to do so– according to the impermanent, materialistic laws of the world. These laws are programmed into our minds throughout our lives by society. They are not inherently "evil," they are simply in opposition with spiritual laws or principles. Some of these material laws or values include excessive consumption, competition, and an over-emphasis on appearances, all of which focus on the external environment. Living in alignment with material values makes the environment our primary focus of attention and source of energy. This creates a pattern of existence that is outward focused, one that moves toward objects for consumption. Most of this is done in an unconscious mode, with the only awareness being an underlying sense of deep emptiness or unworthiness. This is understandable because our real selves don't live outside of us where we're putting all our attention. Therefore, the feeling that something is missing is valid.

In order for an individual to be energized and fulfilled, values must be aligned with the real source of energy, the inner self, which is the home of soul and spirit. Personal alignment consists of coming to know and honor the nature of this place. When this happens, the secondary levels of our being (personality, mind, and body) fall into their natural role, which is that of a container. As a container, our body effortlessly expresses life energy rather than trying to harness energy from outside. Life itself becomes the master, and our physical being becomes the servant. The irony of this reversal is that once proper alignment takes place, our personality, mind and physical body relax and we become more of what we were meant to be: healthy, vibrant, creative individuals living out our gifts. At this point we are inspired to cultivate our natural gifts of expression. Not only do we access a quality and level of energy that can never be available from the world, we also expend much less energy when we are aligned as we were meant to be.

Therefore the first step is to reassess our values and the actions that reflect these values, to bring them into alignment with our spiritual self. To do that we must first look at the conditions under which spirit thrives. There is a place inside each of us where our spirit lives, and with which we need to become familiar and intimate. This place inside of us is often referred to as the inner or eternal or essential self. For me and for many others, the physical location of my essential self is my abdomen. This is where my attention goes when I want to connect to my spirit.

To reverse the flow of energy from outside in to inside out, we need to get to know this inner self that we can't see. As we learn more about the conditions that allow spirit to thrive and grow we can begin to cultivate those conditions within the context of our own lives. The conditions that allow life/spirit to flow are referred to as principles. Just as the principle of photosynthesis states that plants need light to grow, there are principles that are necessary to support the flow of life and spirit through our being.

The nature of spirit is timelessness, abundance, connectedness, and intelligence. If we are in tune with these qualities then life will reveal itself in the simplest of moments. Getting in tune with these qualities brings us closer to our essential nature, because spirit is who we are at the deepest level.

Timelessness

Our soul and spirit live in a timeless realm, only perceptible in the present moment. In order to reap the full energizing properties of this realm we must spend at least a portion of our day in a timeless state of mind. Where is your mind at this moment? Is it divided between this book and something else of interest? To appreciate this concept, think back to a time when you were fully present in any one moment. Perhaps it was a time when you were in a garden or at the ocean, and the energy of the environment was powerful enough to capture your full attention. This is a healing space. It is a moment when all your energy is pulled back into the body only to reveal the true nature of life. Did you have a revelation? Did you feel inspired, directed and whole? A friend of mine recently returned from a trip to Mexico. She told me that several times throughout the week she found herself with a completely clear mind! Once it lasted for nearly twenty minutes before she started thinking again, "Wow, my mind is completely clear." When I asked her how she attained this difficult but rewarding state of clarity, she said it came as she watched a pod of dolphins. She went on to describe five full-grown dolphins and one baby swimming and playing in the ocean for hours on end. All the miscellaneous, erratic thoughts that fill her mind each day left, as she became completely focused on the sight of the dolphins swimming back and forth, the feel of the sun on her skin, and the breeze that was keeping her cool. Weeks later, she is able to reflect on that stillness and realize what a precious gift it was.

There are many ways to attain this quality of mind. Some people are able to go into a timeless realm while playing a musical instrument; others need to sit and consciously breath while going into a meditative state. One naturally falls into a timeless realm when thinking activity ceases. However, how one accesses a state of timelessness is not important–accessing it on a daily basis is very important. Experiencing pure, present-moment existence for even a moment of each day connects us to our source and infuses us with fresh energy.

Often, however, we are strung out in the land of time. It is easy to recognize when a person is spreading her energy thinly over time. You can see a dazed look in her eyes as she walks around partially conscious. This happens to all of us from time to time. In fact, it is likely what got me into this field of spirituality and psychology. When I was younger I was so strung out that I would routinely get in car accidents! It is scary to think about the danger I was putting myself in as a result of being preoccupied.

Here, in an unaware state of consciousness, we do not reap the immense benefits of the eternal world of timelessness. When our attention is dwelling in the past or tossed into the future, we become literally diluted as we spread our energy thinly across our concerns. Being strung out in time is a fundamental characteristic of life in the modern world. It is as if we have tricked ourselves into believing that we have control over whatever it is we are thinking about, when in actuality, control over the present moment is lost.

Power is directed by our attention. For example, if our attention is on a traumatic event that occurred a year ago, our personal power goes in that direction. This keeps the event alive in our psyche. Another part of our attention may be on a special event that we are going to attend next week, while still another part of our attention is focused on the friend that are talking to in the present moment. How much of you is really present in the conversation with the friend? Have you ever experienced an interaction with a person who is totally present? The feeling is unmistakable. In fact, it feels like a gift, because this person is really there, hearing and feeling every word you say. The ability to completely listen *and* hear what another is saying is the natural result of being focused on the present moment. In comparison, a conversation with an individual who is strung out in time wastes the energy of both parties, and usually feels unfulfilling for both. Rather than crackling with currents of electricity, the conversation hums along barely loud enough to keep anyone's attention.

If our essential self is by nature timeless and only exists in the here and now, we must take care of ourselves in a way that frees us to become focused on the present. We have the ability to make this kind of experience part of our daily life. Even an instant of being fully present provides an immense amount of energy to carry us throughout the day. Imagine having twenty minutes of present moment existence! The energy that comes from the present has a quality that is unforgettable and incredibly nourishing. This is "real" energy, energy that is not simply borrowed from the environment, but given as part of the gift of life. The person who is a whole container expressing creative, spiritual energy in the moment is literally bringing fresh life and energy into their world.

Each morning when I wake up I spend at least a few minutes quieting my mind (Ideally I spend a half-hour, but my precious toddler needs me at times and so I try to keep a light attitude about the amount of time.) I begin by breathing deeply and slowly for about five breaths. This is usually enough to bring my awareness to my breath and body. After the deep breathing, I breathe normally and simply sit with my eyes closed. My goal is to attain a clear mind for at least an instant, ideally longer. I envision a clear mind like a lake with no ripples. Something wonderful happens when we slow ourselves down enough to perceive a moment between thoughts. Until you consciously experience a moment between thoughts, it is difficult to imagine. Arriving at this place is one of the goals of a meditation practice, though it can and does occur at other times, such as the experience my friend had with the dolphins. The moment my mind becomes still energy explodes through every cell of my body. It is as if the clarity made room for a rush of nourishment in the form of spirit or life energy. These moments of stillness carry me through my day. I'm given vision and insight when working with a client, or patience with my daughter after a long day. My favorite gift is when I walk outside and see the trees glistening and the sky a vibrant blue. It is as if I have been given another set of eyes, and I believe I have. They are spiritual eyes. Unfortunately, most of the time I still see with my material eyes. With these eyes I really don't see at all; rather I am in my busy mind, thinking about things that may or may not be important.

Stilling the mind and sinking into the present is a proactive way of supporting our spiritual and mental health, just as exercise supports our physical health. Combining the breathing with the stillness or meditation is enormously helpful. As you go through your day you can use conscious deep breathing to take you to a quiet place when stress or frustration arises. Because you have taught your body to associate conscious breathing with relaxation, the body will automatically respond physiologically to the breathing.

If you are new to this practice, allow yourself time to learn it. Just because you don't feel the effects immediately doesn't mean it is not working. I hear people say, "I can't do it, my mind thinks too much." Well then, just practice. Every day, breathe and be as still as you can. As with every skill, it takes time to develop proficiency. Breathing and sitting still works from the very beginning to start clearing away static and congestion in the psyche. If you don't perceive the stillness for a while, it's because you have a lot to clear away! Be easy on yourself and, as Nike would say, "Just Do It."

Abundance

Internally derived energy is also abundant and unlimited as opposed to finite. If we are being fueled at a spiritual level, the fuel directs us and provides sustaining energy that is impossible to achieve from the environment. Energy from the environment is borrowed; it always has to be paid back in one form or another. An afternoon cup of coffee or piece of candy provides a short-lived boost that declines by early evening. This roller coaster of endless highs and lows occurs every time we consume external energy to excess. We need food, sleep, material goods, and each other to function in this world. However, if any of these are relied upon beyond basic necessity, the excess will block the flow of creative energy expressed from within. Imagine a hose that runs continuously. If the hose reversed the flow in an attempt to expediently obtain water from a nearby puddle, it would block the flow of water from its source and become confused (assuming it had a rational mind) regarding its proper function. This is what happens when we consume in excess. In our feeding frenzy, we forget that our true function and ultimate source of fulfillment comes from expressing the life energy that flows from within.

There are many reasons why we choose to rely on energy from "outside." One of the primary reasons is that the flow of authentic expression is already partially blocked by emotional residue from earlier experiences. Later we will look at ways to release those blocks. For now, it is sufficient to know that other than societal training, bad habits, or addictions, emotional blocks are the primary reason that people over-rely on external energy. Chasing external energy can sometimes be a distraction to keep us from feeling pain or numbness that is present within our bodies.

The energy found within is abundant—in fact it is limitless and is waiting to animate your being with life. When spirit is in charge there is enough of everything to go around. Enough love, enough money, enough jobs or whatever it is that we desire to have in this world. The mere requirement is that we follow the rules of life, not the rules of materialism. Life's purpose is to express itself freely. We are simply a *means* to that end, not the end result. The first step in supporting the expression of life is to adjust our belief system accordingly, which we will explore in greater depth in the next section. We need to remember that in giving we receive and in hoarding we suffer. That is because the mind in a giving state is open, and life flows freely and creatively through an open vessel. If we are choosing not to adopt an open orientation, we are choosing to cut ourselves off from our deeper self. If there is a block, life will wait patiently until the block is removed and it can flow again, gracing us with many gifts in the process. Often we can remove a block simply by remembering our purpose of expressing life, love, or spirit. The mere willingness to be a vessel for pure self-expression activates the mind and body on all levels to begin preparing for this sacred journey. Having an understanding of the principles of true self-expression helps us to keep our thoughts and actions in alignment with those principles. For example, if I feel I am not receiving enough support from people around me, it is probably that I am closed off to them, thereby blocking my own spirit, which is my real source of support.

Unified

When two people feel a deep connection between them, the experience is an illustration of the way the eternal self is unified with all of life. We are all connected with a force that is hard to describe. We appear to be completely separate from one another. This belief is reinforced by our language and by western culture's emphasis on individual independence. But each of us knows on some level that we are all connected at the level of spirit. Although there is so much about each of us that is different, this unified aspect of spirit is what creates the link that ties us all together. This ribbon of life brings about what Jung referred to as synchronicity. Things in the outer world come together at the same time that they are being contemplated in the inner world. The connected feeling that reassures us that we are not standing alone in this world comes to us as a gift when we spend time getting in touch with the spiritual part of ourselves–the part that is joined with all of life.

We are most aware of this ultimate connection when we are able to put aside judgements and preconceived notions about one another. This aspect of life thrives best when we remain in non-judgment of each other. Non-judgement allows life to move freely, energizing our senses and nourishing the soul. Nothing blocks the natural flow of spirit quicker than a judgment. Judging another human being paralyzes the soul, not to mention the hurtful effect it has on the person who's being judged. Despite these effects, making judgments seems to be a habit that is often condoned by society. Habit is the key word here—nearly everything that is counterproductive to the flow of life is simply a habit that can be modified with the right inspiration, and judgement is a good example. In a heightened state of awareness, we can actually feel our energy become heavier with every dark word or thought about another person. Keeping the mind open to shifts in energy relating to changing thoughts can provide the inspiration to alter our perception. We can choose to float lightly in our being or be chained to the underground laden with judgmental feelings.

I often use this principle to explain why setting boundaries in everyday life benefits all who are involved. Often times, when this principle of connectedness is embraced, people begin to feel that they need to do more for other people. It can be difficult to navigate through the fine line of connection and separation in our relationships. When a client comes to me and says "My friend needs me—but I just can't do it anymore!" that is a sure sign that the person is confused about the balance between boundaries and compassion.

When you feel the "need" to put others first at your expense, no one is winning and everyone is suffering. The reason for this is that we are all connected at the level of spirit, yet we are each responsible for nourishing ourselves from the level of our source (spirit), rather than from other people. Therefore, when my client does so much for her friend that she begins to feel drained and resentful, it is certain that her friend is being carried by her or relying on her for energy. This pattern of relying on other people for energy unwittingly undermines the friend's self-esteem (a reflection of the degree to which a person is aware and connected to his or her own source of life energy.) Think of this scenario in terms of spiritual energy. If there is a subtle force that is who we are at the most basic level and this force is everywhere, then the person who is sharing her force with her friend is keeping her friend from being aware of her own source. This is where the concept of enabling comes from. The key is this: if we are feeling resentful about something were doing for another person, we are not doing anyone any favors. The feeling of resentment is telling you to set a boundary or say no to some or all of what is occurring. That way your energy will not be drained by another person and the other person will learn how to tap into her own source of energy!

Intelligence

Our spiritual nature is intelligent. Spending time in the stillness of the soul allows one to be touched by the all-knowing aspect of life. Becoming aligned with this universal intelligence is, for me, one of the biggest rewards associated with doing spiritual work. Knowing that all the information I need comes not from my brain, but from a larger force that is connected to all of life, takes away some of the pressure that I used to put upon myself. Allowing ourselves to receive this gift of knowledge and information from an enlarged perspective is truly awesome. It can be challenging at first, however, to admit that one does not have all the answers. After that moment of ego-panic, it becomes pure relief, as we realize we don't *need* to have all the answers. This is where the virtue of humility comes in–to be able to able to step aside, still the mind and allow pure wisdom and direction emerge.

Changing our frame of reference to one of openness is necessary to receive the gifts of knowledge, direction, and insight. The catch is that maintaining an open, receptive mind is totally the opposite of what we are taught. We learn phrases such as, "Always be on your toes", and "Think things through." The messages become so ingrained that to change the posturing of our mind we must completely retrain ourselves. Ultimately, developing a receptive state of mind involves suspending our habitual thoughts so that information from the river of life is able to bubble up and be perceived. At times, it is useful to prepare to listen by opening your mind as if you are going to listen to another person, only the person you are preparing to listen to is you. It is a different level of you that cannot be heard over random mind-chatter, which is why it helps to put the mind in listening mode—the place that does not know what is going to be said, but is quietly and eagerly waiting. As I write, life is expressing itself through me onto this page. Just prior to sitting down to the computer, my mind was running in circles over a bad haircut I had just received. While a bad haircut is clearly not a life-changing situation, the reality is that my mind was torn away from the present moment with irrelevant, obsessive thoughts about some uneven edges at my neckline that would take a magnifying glass for the average person to spot. As I closed my eyes to become centered for writing, I was able to see what my mental ruminating was doing. In my mind I saw an image of a strip of cloth tied so tightly around my waist that it was literally squeezing the life out of me. There was no life coming in, and surely there was no life going out. I was putting limiting thoughts on top of expansive, unlimited information that was ready to flow naturally once I was ready to allow it.

The objective is to make a clear path through which intelligent energy can flow. Limited thinking blocks true knowledge and causes us to wither, as would a flower if it were searching for water through its petals rather than its roots. When you find yourself dwelling on meaningless thoughts about yourself or someone else, be still for a moment and relax into the present moment. Close your eyes and focus on your breathing. Soon your mind will clear. (This will be easier to do if you practice conscious breathing or meditation regularly.) The blocks to life will melt in the silence. When you relax into the present moment with the mind open and still, information will present itself in the form of subtle feelings, insights, and answers. When you drop beneath your racing thoughts you will visit the home of your soul, and spiritual information can bubble up to the surface of your awareness. Because spiritual knowledge is embedded in the source of all life, this spiritual knowledge carries with it the "bigger picture." For me, as I was dwelling on my bad haircut, when I stilled my mind and became centered the bigger picture emerged to show me that who I am is expansive and calm, rather than constricted and distracted. This was a fairly easy transition to make because there wasn't a lot of emotion attached to my thoughts about my hair. It was simply an annoying distraction. When a situation brings with it a lot of emotion, the process of relaxing into our true, more expansive self might require a greater effort, such as going for a walk or engaging in some other activity that will help shift your energy and create enough stillness to perceive the truth from your deeper self.

The intelligence and insight that come from our spiritual nature reflect all aspects of a given situation or relationship because the knowledge is coming from a source that is connected to all of life. Therefore, a decision based on guidance from your inner self will be for the good and growth of everyone. At times, a resounding "NO" will be the answer to a decision in question. It is much easier to say, "I don't feel comfortable going forward at this time," when you know your "NO" benefits everyone involved and not just yourself.

Whether this "NO" refers to a marriage proposal, a job offer, or simply to a slice of cheesecake, it becomes an answer born of conviction deeper than the tangible factors on which most decisions are based.

It takes time to develop the ability to allow one's deeper self, and the intelligence that flows from it, to run the show. At first, surrendering to the subtle wisdom of the inner self feels like giving up the reins that control the direction in which life moves. Instead of a quick, loud voice coming from the limited mind, a subtle feeling of affirmation or uneasiness reveals itself. It is easy to override the unfamiliar voice of spirit that speaks in symbols and feelings that we have been taught to ignore. Over time, however, we can learn to quiet our mind and wait for the voice of truth to respond. Each time we heed inner wisdom the voice becomes louder, and the feelings easier to recognize and honor. Some people report that they actually hear words telling them what to do. As I mentioned before, I have had powerful experiences in which I actually heard a voice inside my head. I find that listening to my inner voice is a lot like skiing, shifting my attention, as I do my weight, from one side to the other to maintain balance and flow. Alternately, I check in with my intuitive center (my gut) and my mind (my head), to navigate through the day consciously, on a moment by moment basis. If I have an uneasy feeling from my gut, I stop and wait until I know how to proceed. This process is subtle and the information that I receive comes mostly in feelings, though the feelings are very strong and, if ignored, they become even stronger until they are acknowledged. Every now and again I am blessed with the clarity of a voice, which brings an incredible sense of calm that reassures me of its source.

Andrea is an old friend, who was in the process of making a decision about buying a condominium in an area that was not yet established, although expectations were that it would develop into an up-market urban center. She listed for me the pros and cons, along with many "ifs." We discussed the implications of making a decision without awareness, and I encouraged her to look within herself for the subtle feelings that create a sense of conviction about a decision. Ultimately, I explained, to get a clear answer she needed to put down her pencil and paper and become still enough to sense the wisdom of her inner self. The next day, I received a call from Andrea who told me that she received a resounding "YES" to her question of whether or not she should buy. This was the answer she wanted all along, but now she had the conviction to move forward despite the risks.

If Andrea had made a different decision, would the world have come to an end? No, however the cost of making a decision that is contrary to the urging of the inner self can create a karmic mess that takes extra energy to clean up.

The gifts we receive from honoring our essential nature are inner peace, genuine self-esteem, and nurturing beyond imagination. In order to receive these gifts we must live in alignment with the above life principles (timelessness, abundance, connectedness, intellegence) that govern the eternal world of soul and spirit. Being aware of these principles is only the first step. Living them is step two, and begins by spending time in the unseen world. This world lives below the level of our thoughts. I once heard Jungian analyst Marion Woodman say that she does not take any clients who are not willing to spend an hour a day on inner work. She believes that this is a small commitment to make in order to receive the gifts that come from honoring oneself.

Each of us must start from where we are, at this moment. If you are reading this book, it is likely that you are already aware of the benefits of slowing down long enough to hear your inner voice. Our inner self blossoms with attention. Even one moment a day given to our deeper self will bring more peace, insight and laughter into your day. Over time, alignment becomes much easier, because as the inner self grows it is only natural to relax and let it guide us. Doors open and life shifts from being an uphill struggle to a journey down a beautiful stream.

By respecting these already established laws, rather than making our own, the conditions are present for spirit to flow forth unobstructed through the soul, then the mind and finally the body. The result is a perfectly unique act of creation. Whether this act of creation is a sentence made up of words, a song or a piece of art, it will always contain elements of eternal spirit and unique soul. If we are not aware, or choose to ignore the conditions in which spirit thrives, it will wait until we create a supportive environment before revealing itself by dancing in our presence. As we will see later, this process unfolds in its own time, and effects each of us very differently. How we are affected depends upon our unique gifts and specific unresolved energy pockets that are released as a result of a steady stream of energy moving through the body.

Aligning Your Mind with the Nature of Life

THINKING IS A NORMAL AND AUTOMATIC function of our physical body and is absolutely required to function in this world. The mind, however, has different levels of thought. We can best utilize each level when we are aware of it's purpose. Our brain monitors the body and keeps us balanced and in tune with the world around us. The deeper mind, which is connected to the soul and spirit within, offers guidance and direction that serves all levels of our being as well as serving those around us. To base our decisions on the part of the brain that monitors data and makes practical decisions is to limit our experience to the familiar. Repetition and boredom result when we never get deeper than the analytical part of the brain. Spending time in solitude and practicing ongoing awareness helps to identify when we need to go beyond our habitual mode of repetitive thoughts into a more creative and receptive state of mind.

Reversing the flow of energy from outside-in to inside-out calls for an evaluation of the way we think about life and the world around us. Many of the beliefs that govern our daily lives are actually inconsistent with the true nature of life, because they are based on a model that values competition and consumption rather than expression and abundance, which are the natural laws of life. These inconsistent beliefs result in thoughts that actually block self-expression. Self-expression in its various forms is like water running down a stream; if the water is blocked by a dam, life around the stream withers and dies. Therefore, thoughts and actions that are based on inaccurate beliefs block your life source from entering the world, simultaneously cutting off nourishment to yourself and the surrounding world.

Our behaviors follow our beliefs, and depending upon the paradigm one is operating under, behaviors can either be self-defeating or self-honoring. With some awareness of life-promoting principles, it is not difficult to bring our thoughts and behaviors into alignment with these principles so that we are working in harmony with life co-creating our existence.

Below are some of the ways we can modify our thoughts and behaviors to be in line with our essential nature.

Minimal Planning

In Western society we are taught to plan. Planning is viewed as the healthy, responsible thing to do in life. Making plans is an essential part of living a productive life. However, making too many plans diminishes the directive power of our inner selves. Our deeper self has knowledge of what is best for us on all levels, not simply at the level of personality. The personality sees only one perspective and therefore does not have access to all the information that is required to make a decision that honors the flow of spirit.

To be in alignment with the nature of life, planning needs to be deliberate and minimal so that we can free ourselves to act spontaneously as directed by our inner self. Excessive planning and overbooking create a chronic distraction from the core self and therefore block spiritual expression. Being chronically busy in and of itself can be an addiction, as we all know. Regardless of the form of an addiction, it creates a separation between one's personality and one's essence.

Minimal planning allows us to honor the aspect of self that lives only in the present moment. Our higher self, if allowed, will provide us with specific direction on a daily basis to help us achieve our goals. That is not to say that structure in one's daily activities is not useful. In fact, we need to have some structure and discipline in order for the mind and body to hold the fullness of our essence. When planning your day, it is a good rule of thumb to do only a skeletal plan. Make a list of what needs to get done along with some firm appointments but leave some room for variation. Try not to get agitated when things are not going exactly according to plan. Keep in mind that there are no accidents, and that the day may actually be working out better than the way we had planned it ourselves.

Time to Be Still

Along with minimal planning, it is important to take time each day to nurture and nourish the inner self by allowing the mind to become still. Time spent being quiet creates order in the self and puts the soul and spirit in charge. In a sense, taking this time informs the personality and body that direction will come from within. It also creates a clear path of communication so that inner direction for and throughout the day can be received. Ideally, it's best to take time for stillness in the morning, so the day begins with mental clarity and inner peace. Meditation (deliberately stilling the mind) cultivates an awareness of the inner self, allowing the mind to slow down so that the higher self can direct the day. If you find it difficult to sit quietly, then try exercising, writing in a journal, or any other activity that you do in solitude to help you connect with your inner self. An hour a day doing any combination of these things is ideal, although even five minutes will create an intention that puts you on the right track at the start of a day.

Julia Cameron, artist and author of *The Artist's Way*, recommends a good dose of writing each day. She refers to this process as "morning pages." The idea is to rise each morning and hand-write three pages of anything that comes to mind. Ms. Cameron uses writing in this way as one form of meditation. I have found it to be emotionally therapeutic. Writing in the morning is also an excellent way to reflect on dreams from the previous night. Many times highly informative dreams evaporate in the light of day if they are not recorded upon waking. In addition, the technique is a valuable way to process feelings so that they do not build up and congest our inner world. Finally, daily writing results in a natural prioritizing of the day, which prevents valuable time and energy from slipping through our hands.

Allowing the priorities of your day to emerge in a quiet, thoughtful way is much different from frantically writing things in a day-timer. A more reflective approach allows insights to emerge–all of a sudden you may think to yourself, "I do not want to spend my time attending this event because it will deplete rather than nourish my being." Time takes on a whole new dimension when viewed from the inside out. A new relationship between time and energy is born. Time spent on tasks that are not assigned by spirit literally require an expenditure of available energy. Conversely, time spent consciously has the effect of invigorating and nourishing us.

Minimal Thinking

You are on your way to work thinking about how much money you have in your checking account and whether it is enough for the weekend getaway that you have planned–which reminds you that you still have to get your coat back from the dry cleaners because it will likely be cold–which leads you to wonder, "does my nephew still have a cold? I should call them and see what's going on"

This is the way our minds work–they are constantly busy. In the meantime, while you're having all of these erratic thoughts, you pass the bright orange leaves on the autumn trees without ever noticing them and forget to waive at the nice person who let you go in front of them. **Excessive thinking distracts us from life.**

Of the incredible number of thoughts that run through our minds each day, a large percentage of them are repetitive. This type of processing is more like ruminating, or possibly even obsessing, than actual thinking. In order to align the mind with the inner self, we must shift from thinking thoughts to receiving information. Obsessive thinking can become an addiction, a way to avoid your emotions by running around in circles in your mind. It is said that it takes a very intelligent person to be neurotic. It is easy for a neurotic person to appear to have it all together, and it takes a much closer look to perceive the chaotic thinking that is actually taking place below the "together" surface.

The only way to get beyond addictive or neurotic thinking is to acknowledge that there is another level of awareness and to shift our attention to receiving information from a deeper level of the mind. Learning to be receptive to insights from one's higher spiritual self is a matter of disciplining the mind, almost like expanding the experience of meditation into daily living. Earlier (in the section on "Timeless") we discussed the technique of using conscious breathing with meditation or stillness in the morning and then invoking the same stillness later in the day by simply doing the breathing part as needed. You can use the same technique to help you tune in to your inner self. With practice, you will be able to adopt a quiet or receptive state of mind as easily as you turn your head. The mind simply clicks into a different mode, becoming sure and focused rather than scattered.

Abundance vs. Competition

Competition is another paradigm that, although ingrained into the fabric of society, does not support holistic thinking. In truth, at the deepest, most enduring part of ourselves, we are connected with one another. When one person wins it benefits all of us. Being aligned with the nature of spirit calls for a shift in thinking to accommodate this truth. Competing with one another is in direct opposition to the flow of life. The flow of life would have us all win and be happy. The true nature of life or spirit, if embraced, multiplies as it is received. Therefore, if one of us is truly blessed with anything, we are all essentially blessed.

Unfortunately, most of western culture embraces a very different understanding of competition. We are taught that we must fight and be tough to get to the top. We are taught that we must be better than other people; this is a terrible position to be in–trying to convince ourselves that we are better than others, all the while knowing deep down that we are not and never will be. All the energy expended trying to convince ourselves and the rest of the world can be saved by acknowledging the simple truth that we are all ONE.

Once the myth of competition is dissolved, life shifts once again. We relax into the truth of who we are and become radiant. No longer does the strain of trying to stand out get in the way of real beauty, charm, intelligence, and talent. The oxymoron is that when we *strive* to be beautiful, intelligent, and so forth, the beauty of the natural self becomes blocked. In this case, we may appear successful or beautiful on the surface, but at some level we feel as though we are faking it, and others can feel it as well. When we relax into who we are—a unique vessel that expresses the same spirit that all others express—reservoirs of energy will be released. When we try to manufacture an outer self that is somehow "the best," energy that was meant to flow forth in creativity becomes stagnant. When we focus on true self-expression, rather than outer molding, that energy flows freely. Paradoxically, this is also when we can perform at our best, and share our unique gifts. It is easy to spot a person who is radiant from the inside out as opposed to one who is trying to mold themselves from the outside in. The former is the one relaxing in the true confidence of their gifts and shining with the undeniable radiance of spirit.

Start monitoring your thoughts. Do you feel the urge to compete in certain situations? If so, challenge that urge or reformat it to compete simply with yourself. Often, the simple acknowledgment that we are all one at the deepest level creates an immediate lift and an overall feeling of relaxation. Self-assurance replaces self-doubt, and the whole world can sense the change. Uphill maneuvering is replaced with gentle gliding when our self-assurance comes from knowing that everyone, including oneself, is special in a unique way. Eventually, thoughts of competition become waves of appreciation for the uniqueness within each person we encounter. This is much like the feeling that comes to us each time we see a newborn baby and know that he or she is completely and totally precious without even trying.

Body Alignment

As we begin to embrace our spiritual nature as the fundamental source of energy and life, the view of the body begins to shift. Before, most of your attention was focused on the part of you that the world can see. Now it is viewed as a functional container through which you embrace and express life. Your body is animated with spirit to the extent that you view it as a means of expression rather than an object in and of itself. Now, rather than decorating the body exclusively in the name of society's definition of beauty, clothes and ornaments are used to symbolize the inner self and accentuate the radiance that is released from within.

The body is meant to be a container and a vessel for energy, though in many cases, it is not serving its true function. We ignore our bodies in favor of the glorious mind. The mind is glorious, though on its own it is no more than a pot full of unrealized ideals and imprisoning judgments. In harmony with the body, the mind is the originator of dreams. It takes the body to be able to hold those dreams within its cells and in the holding they become reality.

Looking at the body as a means of expression entails taking an inventory of perceptions and behaviors that get in the way of spiritual expression. Creative energy is expressed only when we can contain it. If we have not allowed ourselves to embrace spiritual energy, it is because we have perceived the source of life as originating outside of ourselves. At some level, we perceive our bodies as dark and sinful, and spirit as light and somewhat unattainable. In order to find ourselves, we must go through the process of reclaiming our bodies, and the spirit that we have placed outside of ourselves must be welcomed back to live within our cells. By bringing in light, all hidden parts of ourselves come to the surface, at which time anything that is not in alignment with the core self can be released. This process of integration usually creates some discomfort in the body while the rejected parts of ourselves are reclaimed and felt. The sharp sting of each piece of darkness that is brought into the daylight of spirit is nothing compared to the ongoing heaviness and pressure of keeping those parts of us hidden.

In our culture, the body has been emphasized in a way that is not in alignment with optimal functioning. So far, we have talked about reordering our values so that spirit and soul are leading the mind and body. We tend to both undervalue and overvalue our bodies. Our body is our most fundamental means of communication and self-expression. This is monumental–because of our bodies we are able to interact, love, and live with each other in a human capacity. At the same time, we treat our body as if its sole purpose is to serve us by giving us pleasure through food, alcohol, sex, and so forth. While it's fine to derive pleasure through our senses, putting too much focus on pleasure in and of itself ignores the sacredness of the body. By balancing the body through spiritual, mental, and physical alignment, we allow it to do its job, which is to contain and express our essential self! That is a huge job, but the body is completely equipped and willing if we give it the care and respect it needs.

We are finding now that intelligence isn't just a product of the brain. More accurately, it lives in every living cell of the "mind-body." At this point in time, it is necessary to make a shift in the way we view the mind. This new view of the mind should encompass the body, spirit, and soul. We sometimes forget that the rational mind does not run the show on its own. The body, spirit, and soul work in conjunction with the rational mind to guide us moment by moment. The body is an intelligent organism, that when properly maintained, is able to carry the energy of spirit in each of its cells. When the rational mind, body, soul, and spirit are in alignment with each other, life flows beautifully, nourishing one's being and the surrounding world simultaneously.

The key point is that the body is a container, a vessel, a means of self-expression, and an alive, intelligent organism that instinctively knows how to do its job. To view one's body solely as an object to be manipulated and beautified is to disregard its true function, putting other gods before God, if you will. To do anything that focuses on glorifying our body without honoring its essence is to actually block spiritual energy from flowing through. If instead, we behave in ways that allow spirit to express itself through our body, we honor the spirit, soul, mind, and body.

Have you ever noticed someone who appears so comfortable in their own skin that they actually radiate with calm and energy at the same time? Chances are that person is one who has focused on his or her essence, benefiting from the inevitable purification process that naturally accompanies honoring the deepest part of oneself. The benefits of nourishing your essence are threefold: it allows the body to relax and do its job, to express and co-create with life; it creates optimum health in body, because energies are not being blocked; and, finally, honoring our essence creates ultimate beauty, the kind that radiates from within and shimmers for all to see.

Therefore, the task at hand is to allow the body to fulfill its natural function of self-expression. Mostly, this is a very practical endeavor with a bit of intuition and creativity mixed in. The practical portion is to feed the body when it is hungry and give it what it needs in order to be physically balanced (not to satisfy some kind of emotional craving). The same principle applies to all physical requirements, such as exercising moderately and regularly, which allows the body to shake off excess energy and increase blood flow and oxygen intake. The goal is to maintain physical balance by providing opportunities for the body to take in what it needs, and to release and purify excess energy so that it does not turn into illness or anxiety.

The best approach to caring for your body is get to know it and find an overall lifestyle that supports physical health and balance. There is a great deal of literature available to help you. Deepak Chopra's work, including *Perfect Health,* and Andrew Weil's books offer excellent well-rounded approaches to caring for the body. Ultimately however, it is your job to determine what specific foods and activities are best suited to care for your body and its unique needs. I do not recommend jumping on the latest fad or following a prescribed diet for a long period of time, unless it was created specifically for you by a qualified professional. It is useful to read what is available and experiment to see which combinations result in steady energy, clarity of mind, brightness of eyes and skin. Many times weight gain or loss, or anxiety and irritability are the direct result of too little or too much energy flowing through the body. With practice you can cultivate an awareness of your own unique needs for appropriate support and nourishment.

The process of aligning our thoughts and behaviors with the values of soul and spirit, rather than those of society, is actually a process of integration, or creating integrity in our lives. When maintaining a connection with our essential self is made a priority, anything blocking authentic self-expression melts away. The question about how to take care of your body is answered by asking the further question of, "What action will bring me inner-peace?" Many times what will bring us peace is different from what you think you want. You may want to relax on the couch and watch television, but deep down you know that going for a walk will bring you more inner peace. Physical balance supports the flow of life through your body, therefore, what brings balance will bring peace. Once this paradigm is adopted, there is no conflict of interest between the body, the mind, and the soul. Once we shift into alignment, each part of our being desires the same outcome: the expression of life.

When a commitment is made to promote the natural expression of life through our being, emotional and physical purification takes place naturally. At some point you may experience an increased awareness of an old pattern that is causing your energy to become congested. Perhaps you notice an increased sensitivity to its unhealthy or toxic effects. That may be an indication your system is ready to release that old negative pattern. One way to assist this process of purification is to look at all your current behaviors that bring up discomfort or guilt in any form. Guilt keeps us separated from our true self like no other emotion. This is true in part because the process of feeling guilty can itself become addictive. Ironically, the key to breaking our bad habits is to swear off feeling guilty! We somehow believe that guilt is a punishment and will serve the purpose of deterring the behavior in the future. In reality the guilt keeps us stuck in a downward cycle, repeating the same patterns over and over again. Refusing to indulge feelings of guilt around our displeasing behavior creates a space for the behavior to transform. Surprisingly, it can take more willpower to refuse to entertain guilt than to stop the unwanted behavior. Back in my Chicago days when I was devouring information on spirituality while simultaneously devouring the city's entire inventory of scones, I remember listening to a tape of a Kenneth Wapnick, a clinical psychologist and teacher of the book, *A Course in Miracles*. He was talking about food addiction. He spoke about a woman who unconsciously ate bowl after bowl of ice cream, only to feel guilty later. He instructed her that if she felt the need to have some ice cream to eat it in a state of awareness and self-love. It wasn't long before her cravings diminished simply from shifting her frame of mind from guilt to love and acceptance. Once we begin to experience our addictive behavior with an open heart, the power struggle between our "good self" and "bad self" will cease and we can approach life from a unified or integrated perspective.

As we continue to view our habits with compassion we will be in a better position to learn what need the behavior was trying to meet. Most often, with addictive behaviors we are seeking an emotional need, such as self-nurturing (often sought through food) or excitement (often sought through alcohol or drugs.) These and other emotional needs can often be met through connecting with your inner self. Ultimately feeling connected is what we all yearn for and connecting to your own spirit is connecting to all of life, because at this level, we are one. Becoming aware of the unmet need behind the unconscious, addictive behavior often frees us from guilt, and subsequently, the unhealthy behavior.

Exercise

1. Without censoring yourself, have a private brainstorming session and list all behaviors that cause you to feel guilt or a loss of inner peace.
2. Prioritize those behaviors, with those that are the most internally painful at the top of your list, and the ones that cause the least amount of discomfort and guilt at the bottom.
3. Copy the top three onto a separate sheet of paper. Acknowledge that you will allow as much time as you need to release these patterns that are keeping you stuck in guilt.
4. Focus on number one only. Try to discover the emotional or spiritual need that you are seeking through this self-defeating behavior. (For example, nurturing or excitement.)
5. Ask your higher self to gently release the habit in favor of inner peace. Be compassionate with yourself. Adopt an inner orientation of gentle awareness in the presence of the behavior you are releasing.
6. Allow yourself to work on this first area for as long as necessary (potentially weeks, months, or years) until it feels released. Then proceed to number two and three respectively on the list.

It is important to avoid becoming overwhelmed with thinking so that you can follow signals from your body as to which behavior needs to be addressed first. Your body will give you this information through emotion. For example, a friend of mine recently told me that he realized that he needed to quit drinking while driving home the store after buying some beer. As he was driving home, he became aware of his excitement to get home and drink a beer (or six.) The excitement and anticipation was a signal to him that he had a problem. It could have just as easily been anxiety that gave him that information. He could have been anxious sitting at home with no beer available feeling tense and irritable. Every emotion that you experience carries information. A willingness to receive this information is all you need to effectively listen to your body.

Any behavior that causes chronic inner turmoil actually strangles the life right out of us. Life, spirit, and energy flow through calm corridors producing a state of inner peace. A simple way to make life-enhancing choices is to observe the behaviors that leave you with a peaceful, calm feeling inside. Once you realize that the small decisions you make each day directly effect your state of mind, it is natural to make healthy choices. The shame and guilt that often accompanies self-defeating behaviors is not worth the instant pleasure that comes with the indulgence. Drinking a six-pack of beer may be fun for a couple of hours, but as my friend has learned, the loss of deep inner peace for many more hours takes away any fun it brings. From now on, when aligning thoughts and actions with your spiritual self, use inner peace as a compass and it will guide you to a lifestyle that promotes your spiritual, emotional, and physical well being.

Realigning our thoughts and actions with deep spiritual values can be challenging for a short time, though when done for the right reasons (inner peace) it is far easier than maintaining self-defeating behaviors. If changes are taking place in the name of life, then life lends all its strength, endurance, and ease to the process. This is not to say that some form of effort is not needed. However, most of that effort is needed at the very beginning when you first decide to make a change. The initial commitment to do what your heart and soul needs is often the most difficult part. With commitment comes help from the universe if the change is inspired from within.

There will be more discussion later in the book regarding stopping an addiction or a habit that is deeply ingrained. However, once you experience success with any change, faith will emerge as your partner, and help you endure that brief period of uncertainty until the abundant energy of life is freed to flow down its natural corridors.

RESTORING YOUR CONTAINER

Building Our Capacity to Express Pure Life Energy

IN AN IDEAL WORLD, each of us would be clear channels of energy, aligned with our natural self, with nothing blocking radiant self-expression. In addition, each of us is a whole, strong uniquely shaped container with no leaks or cracks that affect its integrity. Ideally that container is animated by spirit, grounded in soul, and expresses our natural gifts with infectious enthusiasm. In reality, most of our containers are badly in need of restoration. Whether it's old baggage blocking the doorways or leaks that not only let the air out but also bring contaminated energy back in, most of us have some serious work to do in order to contain and then express pure, potent life energy without crumbling.

Clearing Emotional Blocks

EMOTIONAL ENERGY IS INTENSE. The feeling of it moving through our body is similar to giving birth to a baby, in that it moves through us and takes on a life of its own. This is the very reason we avoid it: Emotion is life energy and life energy is who we are, which is foreign to the way most of us believe. We are trained to believe that our container–our mind, our personality, our body–is who we are. In reality, who we are is the life that flows through that container.

My dear friend and spiritual sister Bridget recently shared a revelation that she had that relates to this topic. Bridget told me that during her yoga class she was holding a posture that, after a time, caused her legs to shake. She said, "I wanted to just release the posture because it was so uncomfortable. But I didn't, and as soon as the energy moved through my legs, the tension dissolved and I was able to relax in the posture." Bridget realized that this physical energy is the same as emotional energy, and that it is counter-intuitive to stay present to the intensity of energy as it moves through the body. Rather than surrender to either type of energy, it's easier to do the opposite–to run from it. How easy is it to just start yelling at someone or to intellectualize, or go for something to eat or drink or buy. These are the ways that we distract ourselves and, in these distractions, energy that wants and needs to just flow becomes lodged in the body-mind. As emotional congestion mounts, so does mental and physical illness. We become anxious, depressed, or physically ill as the energy, like a stagnant river, becomes toxic.

Feelings that are not expressed or released in the moment become emotional baggage. This baggage literally clutters space and constricts our ability to contain the life we are meant to hold within and express through our being. We all have experienced events that have blown through our lives like a tornado. These and many other small unresolved interactions severely limit our functioning. But what exactly is this unwanted residue? And how do we release it? As a therapist, I know the benefits obtained by using a trusted professional to assess what emotional work needs to be done in order to clear the way to a brighter future. Having also been a client, I know that most of the work happens at home, at work, and with friends, and not in the safe confines of a therapy session. Therefore, it is important to learn techniques you can use on your own, in everyday life, to clear baggage and unwanted clutter out of your psyche.

We are rarely aware of the blocks that inhibit our own spiritual expression. That's because of a built-in defense mechanism that literally projects our unintegrated feelings and other rejected aspects of ourselves onto other people to protect us from seeing them as our own. When raw emotional energy feels too overwhelming to process as it occurs, it is forced into the subcon- subconscious mind. Projection occurs when a later situation triggers the suppressed pocket of unintegrated energy. To defend against the discomfort, our mind then projects the emotion onto the person that activated it, saying, "You are putting this feeling in me." Unless you are extremely aware of your own emotional "hot spots" you are likely to be certain that the emotion you are feeling is in them, but not in yourself. Projections can also contain positive aspects of yourself that are not yet integrated into your awareness, although this discussion will primarily focus on clearing suppressed negative emotions.

This psychological principle of projection is traditionally utilized within the context of psychotherapy and not by individuals to facilitate their own healing. However, integrating projections is a tool that everyone can use to become aware of emotional baggage that needs to be cleared from the psyche.

Each of us is different, with some of us being highly sensitive and others highly resilient. Therefore, one individual may efficiently process a minor trauma while another could be highly effected for years. One thing is certain–just because something is buried does not mean it is gone.

Suppression and subsequently projection happens to all of us at different times, and they are therefore appropriately considered two of the most common and basic defense mechanism. That is why people never get dealt more problems than they can handle, because their psyche won't allow it. In this sense, suppressing intense feelings is a positive and necessary coping skill to temporarily preserve the integrity of the ego. The problem exists when the suppressed emotions try to resurface, and we continue to force them back down. This becomes repression because the emotionally charged energy is being suppressed over and over to avoid the uncomfortable feelings that were not initially allowed to emerge and flow through the body.

Projections occur systematically to remind us at some level that the suppressed energy is present in ourselves. Rather than experience the unpleasant energy, we push it down again and displace it onto those people in our lives who we believe possess similar energy or characteristics. As long as we choose to react to our own buried material by assuming it lies exclusively in other people (that is, we blame others), it will remain below the surface of our awareness. It will continue to manifest itself in different scenarios until we gain the courage to claim it as our own.

Much of our energy is spent maintaining our projections. First, an immense amount of energy is needed to keep an emotional memory suppressed. Second, when we are projecting, streams of energy are directed toward the object of our projection. Take, for example, a woman who was abused as a child. Young children are sensitive and especially prone to suppressing difficult emotions. Therefore, an abused child will likely suppress shame, guilt, fear of abandonment and other feelings that occur in that situation. If, as an adult, she does not examine these feelings she will continue to be attracted to abusive people who activate her suppressed emotions. Once she does the painful work of consciously experiencing her shame and fear, she will no longer attract and be attracted to abusive people.

Projection occurs on many levels. It can also be observed by looking at famous people who carry mass projections. I recently heard Julia Roberts in one of her films in which she plays a famous actress saying, "fame is not real you know" to her co-star who plays an average person. That statement is very true. The effects of fame are not real because they are not enduring. As soon as the public finds someone else more intriguing, the projections are pulled back, and the elevated feeling produced from being intensely famous is gone. I also heard Steven Spielberg in an interview talking about his work. In effect, he shared that as soon as he puts his attention on the fame or the way people think of him, he will lose creativity in his work. I believe that this is why he is able to continue to create amazing work time after time. He makes an active choice not to accept the projections we are sending in his direction and is therefore not subjected to the ups and downs often associated with fame. A musician friend of mine shared this same perspective regarding the music industry. Often a new band will emerge doing very creative work. After that first surge of fame they will focus their energy, not on continuing to do creative work, but on maintaining status quo in a vain attempt to hold on to their fame. The irony is that in identifying with the fame and/or projections, we lose sight of our essence, which is where creative work is originally born. Quickly, people spot a hollow shell and lose interest. If a person has strongly identified with the projection, as was likely the case with Marilyn Monroe, he or she may feel that a loss of fame is equal to a loss of self and no longer find a genuine sense of meaning in life.

What we project onto others, whether it is negative or positive, is an aspect of ourselves that needs to be reclaimed. Therefore, rather than seeing the part of ourselves that is charmingly beautiful or conversely, devilishly interesting, we see it in someone else. You have heard the saying, "Where attention goes, energy flows." this is exactly what is happening with projection. Valuable energy is literally streaming out toward the object of projection.

The energy that is being lost in maintaining suppression is usually replaced by stealing energy from the environment in some way. This can take the form of a subtle or even an acute addiction. These addictions can range from alcoholism to relationship dramas or shopping frenzies. Once we are able to release the blocked energy, spiritual energy is free to flow, and our system no longer craves environmental energy.

This brings up many questions: How do I know what parts of me are suppressed? On whom am I projecting? How do I allow this energy to be released? What will happen when it is released? The answer to all these questions is stored within the body. The body wants to let go of the extra burden of suppressed energy pockets. Often, extra physical weight is shed when emotional baggage is released. This is because it is no longer needed to act as a buffer against the world around us or to the parts of ourselves that we have unwittingly buried. Because the body will be our teacher in this process, a reconnection needs to be established.

The process of clearing emotional blocks leads to a mind-body connection that is not present when emotional baggage is stored. Sensations in the body are often ignored when we are in the habit of repression (blaming the environment for causing our emotions.) It is often easier to ignore messages from the body than to pay attention to the overwhelming emotions that surface. Paying attention, however, is the key to emotional clearing. Comfort and discomfort in the body reveal emotional blocks that need to surface. Focusing on the mind as separate from the body can provide a sort of "blissful ignorance" that allows the work of purification to be postponed for a while. But once you realize that your psyche is attempting to clear emotional congestion, it becomes unbearable to continue living the same way we did before the awareness. When we gain the courage to begin healing, our body will be a teacher in this clearing process and will take a leading role as we continue to give it the attention needed to do so. After we have attained the first level of personal alignment–aligning with the nature of spirit–emotional purification comes next as the second level of personal alignment.

Without the work of emotional clearing, creative self-expression is limited.

A good way to begin the process of emotional clearing is to take time each day to get acquainted with the many feelings that are present in the body. Be aware of feelings in the stomach, heart, shoulders, and so forth. Do you experience numbness in some areas? Is there tension in other areas? The numbness can be as telling as the tension. Every type of feeling is trying to tell you something. Write down messages you receive from the body. In addition to giving you information about feelings, it will tell you what it needs physically. It may tell you to walk more, to sleep more, or to stop eating chocolate. The messages you receive may be so simple that they're easy to ignore, but making even a tiny change that your body needs could balance your whole system.

You will find that physical cleansing and emotional cleansing occur simultaneously. They go hand in hand because they are virtually the same. Emotions that are not processed at the time they occur become stored in the body as emotionally charged energy. Over time, if you continue to avoid feeling this particular emotion, it will accumulate and take on a life of its own. Periodically it will take over and become explosive and then buried again until the next time. We will discuss how to consciously process these suppressed energy pockets later in this section, though the first step is to become aware of what your body is carrying and what it needs to be healthy and clear. This is accomplished by tuning in to the signals that your body continuously sends.

As you learn to listen to your body, it will begin to let you know about trauma that is ready to be released. This is rarely an effortless process and, unfortunately, it almost always gets messier before it becomes clean. However, there is a wonderful principle that protects us from becoming overwhelmed. That is, you will become aware of each physical or emotional block, one at a time, as it is ready for release. The emotional blocks will be presented to you through your growing awareness of the ways in which you project them onto the world around you.

When an emotional block is ready to be released, you will have the experience of sensing that specific emotion, only you will think it is a justified response to an external event. There are two factors that indicate when we are projecting. The first is repetition. You will experience the same disturbing feeling recurring in different situations. The second indication is the intensity of the feeling. Instead of becoming mildly irritated with your spouse for making a minor mistake, you become enraged. Rather than feeling a normal sadness over someone canceling plans to get together, you feel despair. Repetition and intensity are symptoms that will help to differentiate between appropriate feelings in response to a given situation and extreme reactions that are caused by a projection that has been triggered by an external event.

Even though you have clues that indicate projection is occurring, it can be extremely difficult to be objective enough to take responsibility for your own emotions in these situations. As John Ruskan states in his enlightening book *Emotional Clearing*, "To succeed in processing, you must intellectually accept the condition of suppression-projection as a working axiom, even if you have to do so on faith. As you begin to integrate material that was previously suppressed, the truth will gradually become evident, and you will be astounded as well as fascinated." Therefore, even if we are SURE that what we are perceiving is coming entirely from the other person, it is wise to assume that your own projection is involved in the dynamic. Clarity will be your gift, but only after you have done the work of reintegrating your projection and processing the suppressed emotional energy.

If we view a projection, with all its discomfort and intensity, as an attempt of the psyche to clear away stored debris, we will be in a position to embark on the quickest and most effective way of healing ourselves. Just as the body naturally disposes of waste, the psyche naturally tries to dispose of blocks that keep us congested. Our job is to honor the process, first by becoming aware of what is happening and, second, by being gentle with ourselves while allowing the clearing to take place. This is a challenging process while it is occurring, although the emotional freedom that emerges after only a short time will ease any doubts. The efforts associated with living a conscious life will be well rewarded.

In the midst of experiencing a projection it seems as though what we are seeing is real when, in fact, what we believe to be objective reality is subjective perception. We may talk to people we trust and try to convince them of the validity of our intense feelings about the situation. At some level we know there is more to the scenario than meets the eye; however, most of us are very skilled at protecting ourselves from perceiving our own negative baggage. It takes effort and most of all humility to contemplate that some of what we are seeing may be contained only in our own vision. Keep in mind that projections may be positive as well as negative because the material displaced upon the other person is an aspect of ourselves that we have buried.

When you are in the midst of what you suspect may be a projection the best way to cope is to ride the wave without fighting against it. Rather than trying to stop the flood of emotion, allow yourself to experience and accept the feelings, even though they can be overwhelming and intense. The immediate goal is take care of yourself while not blaming other people for your experience. Blaming is a natural reaction to such overwhelming feelings, but it is self-defeating.

Reacting to the feeling by losing your temper or stuffing it down with food or alcohol will only cause the feeling to be pushed down once again which keeps us emotionally congested. By talking ourselves through the experience and focusing on breathing we allow the feelings to move through the body. Blaming another person or a situation is an attempt to keep the feelings from emerging. This is about as effective as trying to stop a large wave from rolling onto the beach. It will eventually break though. Whether it destroys us our not depends on our ability to ride rather than resist. Once the flood of emotion subsides it is easier to discern how much of the reaction was projection and how much was reality. Once this determination is made, we can respond appropriately in a manner that serves ourselves and the others involved.

There are certain situations that are unacceptable and call for setting a clear boundary such as severing ties with an individual or stating ones truth unequivocally. In these cases the conviction behind your decision will be stronger if you are certain that you're responding to an external event rather than reacting to your internal wounds.

Say, for example, you suppressed the assertive, bold part of yourself as a child. There are many reasons children might do this–most often it would be because they were reprimanded each time they made a strong statement. Years later you meet someone at work that you cannot stand to be around because they are "so pushy." Most of us are unaware of the dynamic of projection, and when we experience a strong feeling about someone, we generally assume the feeling is caused by his or her behavior. Most of the time this causes us to react to that behavior as if our assessment of it were objective, disregarding our tendency to distort and exaggerate the situation through the filter of our clouded perceptions. Our response may take the form of bad-mouthing the "nasty, pushy" person, or we may confront them directly, saying something like, "You always want it your way." Whatever form the reaction takes, the effect is to keep that injured part of us unhealed. This is not to say that we should not communicate a difficulty that we are having with someone, even with the person who is directly involved. We can, however, hold an awareness that a large portion of our reaction may be projection, especially if we have a pattern of being sensitive to this type of behavior. Taking responsibility for the intensity of our reaction does not absolve the other person of their portion of responsibility. There is usually a kernel of reality in our perceptions. The point is that if there weren't something inside of us needing to be released, triggering our emotional response, *we would not obsess* about the other person's behavior. There will always be people who do things that we do not agree with. However, unless some projection is involved we do not go around with a fire burning in our belly over it! It is nearly a guarantee that a projection is lurking if there is a belly fire or any other type of intense bodily reaction involved. This cycle of trigger-projection-reaction could potentially go on forever, and often does, if we do not actively choose to be responsible for our healing. A general lack of unawareness of the nature of projection and healing is the primary reason why these dynamics often continue throughout one's life.

Marion Woodman, a Jungian Analyst who specializes in eating disorders and addictions, uses the phrase "holding the tension of the opposites," in other words, keeping oneself from reacting to an inner impulse even though it causes acute tension in the body. Sitting on the impulse or, more eloquently, holding the tension simultaneously releases suppressed energy and increases will power and self-confidence. The tension we experience when we do not give in to a compulsive desire is the result of energy transmuting into a lighter, more refined energy. Once the pocket of suppressed energy is even slightly diminished, the previous energy needed to keep it contained along with the transformed emotional energy is released, increasing our capacity to contain and express life. The increased strength that comes holding the tension makes the clearing process exponentially easier. One example of this phenomenon is going on a diet. We have all heard people say, "If I could just get started." We all know at some level that the initial act of will is the most difficult. After that, our renewed inner strength often makes it much easier to carry on.

Some indications that a projection has been triggered:
- You are convinced that the other person is absolutely and totally wrong without a shadow of a doubt.
- Your heart is racing, your face turns red, your breathing shallows, your stomach gets immediately upset, (any number or combination of physiological fight or flight responses).

- You keep running into people who do the same thing "to you" and you "hate" that type of person or behavior.

For most people the intense effects of projection occur episodically rather than continually. Therefore, if we can hold off on reacting, the strong impulse will usually pass in a matter of minutes. A portion of the suppressed emotional energy is released every time we do not impulsively react to a situation that brings about some of the physiological responses described above. Instead we can maintain an awareness of our reaction and the possibility that, we may be projecting.

When dealing with an intense trigger that feels out of control, it can be useful to discuss the experience with someone you trust after you have had time to feel and process the initial wave of emotion. Talking with a trusted friend or therapist about your experience can support and facilitate the healing process. Be careful not to share with people who will judge or criticize you, this only invalidates your experience and hinders the process.

Emotions: Is it better to implode or explode?

THERE ARE MIXED MESSAGES IN American society regarding the expression of feelings. Mostly we hear, "Express your feelings no matter what," because to do so is better for the body than holding feelings inside. However, real-time expression of feelings is only ideal if they are feelings that are under your control, and not a tidal wave of compact emotion ready to crash into any person in its path. We need to distinguish between the healthy expression of a natural feeling such as anger, sadness, or grief and an explosion of pent up emotion such as rage. Most people are not trained in the art of transmuting emotional residue. It is easy to get triggered projections confused with natural day-to-day feelings. In the following pages, methods for dealing with intense emotions or triggered projections will be discussed more thoroughly. Ultimately, it is not beneficial to implode (hold emotion in) or explode. We will look at how to transform the emotional energy so that it does not damage anyone, including ourselves.

Because most triggers happen in the context of relationships, they are the primary arena for self-healing. Many recent books have identified intimate relationships as a vehicle to bring both parties to a deeper, more sacred way of life. However, in every relationship that we have, whether it is with our significant other, a sibling, or a co-worker, an opportunity for healing exists. Some relationships provide more opportunities than others do, and you have probably already identified a primary relationship that is fertile with conflict, waiting to be transformed.

To take responsibility for healing your emotional wounds as they are reflected to you by a loved one takes a tremendous amount of humility and dedication. Although doing this difficult and rewarding personal work in the context of an intimate relationship accomplishes the same thing as traditional psychoanalysis in a fraction of the time. The reason for this is that most people only go to analysis for an hour a week. In this hour it is assumed that the client will eventually project unfinished business onto the neutral analyst. Psychoanalysis can be an effective mode of healing, however, the treatment is based on certain variables occurring in a controlled environment. This is not in any way intended to discourage anyone from seeking psychoanalysis or other forms of individual therapy; for some it is essential and for others it is extremely helpful, especially when one is in need of support. Some people, however, may not need the structure of analysis or therapy if the goal is to overcome experiences from the past that are unfortunately alive in our present minds. Each of us has daily opportunities to clear our psyche of emotional blockage in our homes, offices, and with friends. In fact, we can learn how to heal ourselves by becoming aware of our own projections and by learning how to reintegrate them into the psyche.

There are reasons why it is to our benefit to identify and clear our own internal blocks. If projections are not identified and pulled back from their target, the psyche will contain land mines that randomly explode when a hot spot is triggered. We can end up going from job to job or from relationship to relationship, repeatedly experiencing the same unproductive interactions. We are not taught how to identify our own unhealthy patterns of relating, it is more common to blame the other person, to judge, to react, or to leave. Not taking responsibility for our part in difficult relationships, we unconsciously create drama. The situation is not real; it is one person's projection dancing with another person's projection, both blaming the other person entirely. Processing the repressed energy that is projected outward is the key to emotional freedom. After doing this work we are better able to observe other people's behavior without taking it personally, regardless of how irrational they are acting. In addition, other people are more likely to be able to see the destructiveness of their own behavior when we don't feed it with our own reaction, but are clear enough in ourselves to simply reflect their actions back to them. We can only be a mirror if we are clear enough within ourselves so that we do not react emotionally to their behavior, but simply observe it and respond appropriately. The difference between reacting and responding is the measure of deliberate awareness in our behavior. Have you ever done something stupid in the presence of someone who in response just looks at you with compassion? Chances are, almost immediately you were able to see how inappropriate your behavior was. Now imagine doing the exact same absurd thing, but this time the other person reacts by saying "What are you, stupid? I can't believe you just did that." It's likely that you would focus on their inappropriate reaction and forget all about your own mistake.

In the presence of a clear individual who does not engage in the dance of projections, we are able to take responsibility for our behavior and change it. We not only heal ourselves with this process it also provides an opportunity for others to heal in our presence. Joy spontaneously bubbles to the surface of our being when we are no longer controlled by negative emotions such as anger, jealousy, impatience, and boredom.

There are three steps you can take to help identify and pull back your projections. However, any time we deal with emotions that have been pushed down and kept contained for a long time, it is messy work. While written steps are a starting point, they will not define the entire process as it occurs. Part of the process of transforming blocked energy is surrendering to the unfamiliar (and therefore initially scary) experience of emotional energy moving through us. While processing feelings in general can be overwhelming, this is particularly the case with feelings that have been repressed.

STEP ONE

Whenever intense emotions are felt, immediately focus on breathing fully and steadily. Be aware of the feelings but don't attempt to think too much about them while they are engulfing the body. DO NOT REACT. Simply breathe.

STEP TWO

If the intensity of feeling does not pass quickly, continue to consciously breathe while holding *on to* the emotion until you can get to a place where it is safe just to experience what is happening. A simple intermediate explanation may be necessary for the people or person with whom you are interacting. Say something like, "I'm feeling a little overwhelmed right now. I need to take some time to myself." Once you are alone, experience the feelings by going deeper into them. Crying, writing, or drawing may help, or it may be best to simply continue conscious breathing while you focus on the emotion that is present. Eventually the energy will shift or release, and some clarity will begin to emerge.

STEP THREE

Choose how to proceed based on the emergent clarity. Perhaps you will have identified an event that triggered a strong (suppressed) emotional memory. You may decide to simply explain to the other person that when the triggering event occurred an emotional memory was brought up. Or, you may determine that your reaction was the result of an external event that was genuinely hurtful or inappropriate in some way. Most often it is a combination of an inappropriate action bringing up unresolved emotional residue from the past. The task is then to take responsibility for your overreaction, and to communicate your feelings regarding the situation in an appropriate way. In this case you might say something like, "What happened there really upset me, and I know part of my reaction was based on what I have been through in the past. At the same time, I need to share that I feel disrespected when you talk to me that way." In some cases, such as with verbal or physical abuse, a change in the relationship may be necessary. The point is to take action *only* when you can identify how much of the internal emotional reaction was "trigger" and how much was a natural response to an unacceptable situation.

After reading the steps and experiencing the process first hand, it will be helpful to review the steps again. Once you have experienced blocked energy being released as it moves through you, you will be able to work with it using your own thoughts and images. A metaphor may come to you or you may wish to create your own steps. One powerful metaphor is that of fire as a tool for purification. This metaphor is powerful because processing feelings often does feel very much like a fire burning inside.

Projections occur repeatedly until the hidden emotion is fully brought to light. Therefore, once a "hot spot" has been found there's a good chance you'll soon have another chance to identify it the next time it is activated. The best thing we can do when an emotional memory is triggered is to provide emotional safety and support for ourselves. Many times people around us are not able to fully understand the implications and the intensity of our feelings because they are not completely due to the current situation. Often, others may say we are overreacting, and to them it may appear that way. That is why it is especially important that we understand what we need to do for ourselves in order to feel validated, and most importantly, to heal. The emotions that flood our being during these times ARE real energy, and for that reason are valid and need to be treated as such. For example, if a person feels overwhelming grief over a small loss, the overwhelming grief needs to be felt and allowed to happen. It is our way of processing emotion that was too much to handle at an earlier time.

When we reintegrate projections we take responsibility for ourselves in the highest sense. We acknowledge that there is a part of our being that has not been taken care of. Taking care of ourselves emotionally, at this time, becomes a gift we give to ourselves, like eating right or exercising. It is the difference between living our own life or being controlled like a puppet to the reactive energy trapped within the psyche. As long as we avoid this work we make a choice not to be the directors of our own lives. On the other hand, when we are not preoccupied with avoiding and reacting to our own "land mines," we are able to move in a direction that is in alignment with our higher self. Taking this rigorous path ultimately offers inner peace and a clear sense of purposeful direction that leads to goodness of our body, mind, spirit, and the outer world.

Container Repair: Sealing Energy Leaks

When you exist as a clear, strong container, you will be directed to do what glorifies and multiplies life. This is creative self-expression done in the most unique form possible, because each one of us is a unique individual. We have been talking about clearing any blocks to this self-expression. There is another area that must be addressed if we are to be a strong container. For most of us there are cracks or leaks in our energy system which sometimes allow life to drain, pour, or be sucked out of the body physically or emotionally. The goal is to be physically balanced rather than rely on addictive behaviors for energy, and to be emotionally self-sufficient so that we do not rely too heavily on others for personal validation, support, or for our own sense of peace and happiness.

Picture a container with holes in it. It is meant to be solid. It is meant to deliberately express life energy from the inside out. But for many reasons, the container has not been able to develop naturally or has developed cracks over time, making it difficult to carry its own energy. As a result we resort to getting energy in any way possible as a way to alternatively compensate for this lack of energy. Many times these alternatives become addictions. Addictions are a consistent method of supplying the body with energy from the environment rather than from one's spiritual core. Fulfillment is impossible to attain when we fuel ourselves with environmental energy. This is because the supply is limited and never gives that full feeling of true contentment that comes from spiritual energy.

Energy can be drawn from nearly anything in the environment including activities, people, or a substance. Here, we will look at some of the major areas where people are simply exchanging energy, and we will explore a deeper way of life by reversing the flow from "outside in" to "inside out."

Addictions

All addictions are an indirect attempt to energize the body, however, they are the greatest lie in this world. They lie because they promise to provide some sort of relief, and they never do. The energy they provide is short lived and must be continually replenished or it is rapidly depleted leaving you with less energy than you started with. Despite this, our addictions trick us over and over again simply by their power to provide an instant of gratification followed by what seems to be an eternity of despair.

For the purpose of this book, the term "addictive behavior" refers to any behavior that involves pulling energy into the body from the environment rather than expressing it from the core self. This does not include activities such as eating, sleeping, and so forth, when performed in a way that promotes health in the body. Any activity that consumes external energy as a replacement for self-expression is, in my opinion, an energy addiction. Separating and defining all the possible forms that addictions take, such as substance abuse, unhealthy relationships or activities, and even obsessive thinking, is work that has been covered by many authors. Here we will focus on the *cause* of the addictive activity rather than the specific behaviors. The dynamics of an addiction are the same, regardless of what form it takes.

There are many reasons that addictive behavior is unproductive as well as demoralizing. Addictive energy is brought into our body through a hole in the energy system. This hole in the energy system is reinforced each time an external energy source is abused. The addictive behavior eventually creates an efficient vacuum effect that, when activated, pulls energy immediately into the body. This immediacy factor is one of the primary reasons that addictive behavior is so difficult to control. Once your system is conditioned to "getting" energy instantly upon demand, it does not have much interest in accessing the more stable, albeit fulfilling, energy of spirit. This is not to give the impression that spiritual energy is not immediately available. It is always available. However, spiritual energy flows freely and abundantly from within, and is felt most intensely when it has a solid vessel to flow through, and when the flow is not being interrupted by addictive consumption.

We can engage in behaviors that create a strong container to support the consistent existence and expression of spirit. These behaviors include cultivating the virtues under which spirit thrives, such as non-judgment and honesty. The absence of addictive behavior also supports the presence of spiritual energy. This is because when we aren't consuming energy, spiritual energy has an opportunity to bubble up through our being. Finally, quiet time alone gives our spiritual essence a chance to be heard, which always promotes its presence.

As well as the immediacy factor of addictive consumption we also need to look at the control factor. Often it is difficult to let go of the feeling of control that accompanies an energy binge. Whether one is bingeing on food, alcohol, or items at the mall, there is a false sense of security that comes with the ability to plan these consumptive activities. It is certainly difficult for a person who has depended on the intermittent highs of chocolate or vodka to imagine that a sweeter, more fulfilling kind of reality exists. People who are in the habit of planning their highs find it difficult to have faith that those highs will be supplied naturally if allowed. The reason for this is because it is not possible to experience the reality of spiritual energy, its reliable presence and its spontaneity, if one's entire focus is planning that next addictive fix.

One of the factors that reinforces our dependency on addictive rather than spiritual energy is that when we stop an addictive behavior we experience a lull or drop in our energy level. People who quit smoking, for example, can vouch for the undeniable feeling of numbness punctuated by acute cravings as the addictive energy works its way out of their system. During this time it is hard to imagine the peaceful energy that a life based on spiritual energy can bring. There are also social implications that need to be cleaned up if the addiction was severe. Broken relationships, unspoken apologies, and the discomfort associated with having to look at all the areas in our lives that have been ignored. If the dependence on external energy is not fully an addiction but a bouncing from one substance or relationship to another, the clean-up stage may not be as severe. However, the temporary drop in energy is still likely to occur contributing to an underlying lack of faith in a fulfilling life based on spiritual energy.

The numbness, and feelings of boredom and anxiety that occur when an addictive energy source is cut off only lasts for a short time. It is similar to the process of reversing the flow of water in a hose. There will be an adjustment period during which the velocity is interrupted until it begins to flow in the other direction. If we are not aware of this principle it may be tempting to just resume the addictive activity. When they are struggling to diet or quit a bad habit, I often hear people justify their addictive behavior, saying, "Life's too short," or, "We're all gonna die someday." These comments reflect the desire to avoid that temporary lull in energy. It is an uncomfortable feeling, though it always subsides and the benefit of waiting it out is inner transformation or container repair.

By remaining in that dull, gray, boring, uncomfortable place for a time (usually only several days to a week is long enough to feel your energy re-emerge), the flow of energy begins to reverse becoming bright, clear and immensely more exciting and fulfilling. This is the way that leaks or holes in our container are patched. Regardless of the degree of dependency, each time we resist the magnetic pull of the external energy source of choice, the hole that has developed in our container is continually repaired. We know that symptoms of cravings and symptoms of withdrawal are literally the addictive property being released from the body. As each wave of craving is felt but not acted upon, the object of addiction is de-magnetized, thereby bringing the power and energy back into the body where conscious rather than obsessive choices can be made.

If you have ever stopped an addictive habit, you are familiar with the process I am describing. Being aware of this process is half the battle. Each time a crack is repaired in our container we become more empowered. We become strong and self-confident. The trust in ourselves builds until we no longer desire the external, short-lived energy jolts that used to be so precious.

Karma

Buddhist teachings tell us that, according to the law of karma, for every action there is a reaction. The reaction carries the same energetic quality of the original action. Therefore, if we act with hostility or aggression we will attract situations or people that carry those qualities into our lives. Conversely, if we act with kindness or friendliness, we will attract those qualities. Those seeking enlightenment aim to transcend the world of karma. It is believed that once a person is enlightened they will no longer be required to reincarnate.

There are practical implications of karma in relation to making everyday decisions. If it is possible to rise above the effects of karma once enlightenment is attained, what happens when you or I experience a fleeting moment of enlightenment? How many times have you heard a person say that at a certain moment in time they felt connected with all of life? Because this is my passion, I have these types of discussions frequently. It surprised me however, when last spring I was teaching a class and I asked how many people in the class had an experience where they felt completely spiritually connected. About 80% of the class raised their hands! One student explained that while in the woods, she began to see things around her differently—as if the trees and shrubs were shimmering. She told us that her vision remained this way for several days, and that her perception of the world is still radically altered. This was amazing to me. I live for these stories. It is as if we are all having these moments, but not talking about them openly because they are so private and sacred.

It is my view that when we are perfectly aligned with our essential spiritual self we are in an enlightened state. What, then, are the karmic effects of those moments?

None.

When we are aligned with our spiritual self and relatively clear within, we experience more and more of these moments. When self-expression occurs in a state of total alignment, it is karma free—beyond time and without a trailing effect. I believe that these expressions are born out of eternity (timelessness) and remain there, completely free of residue or effect. These moments reinforce our authentic self and transport us closer to our source.

Karma then, simply put, is action without total awareness. Unconscious action creates an energetic trail that will eventually need to be undone through the process of experiencing the feelings associated with the effects of the action. Not only is it essential to experience the effects consciously, it is also essential that we do not react to the effects, thereby creating additional karma. I am aware that this perspective is different from the traditional view of karma; it is more centered on the effects of our actions in the here and now.

Living consciously is the difference between living your life and having your life lived for you. If life seems to be a constant challenge on an inclined treadmill, it may be that you have karma that needs to be burned off. In many respects, burning off karma is like paying a debt. It is the interest due long after the loan has been satisfied.

Taking responsibility for a bad decision and making a change to make a better decision is the most important step. Decision made apart from spirit (unconscious choices), often leave a messy trail that needs to be cleaned up even after making a more aware and conscious choice. This explains why an alcoholic of twenty years continues to encounter roadblocks after ceasing to drink. I use the example of addiction because this is the most extreme form of unconscious behavior. Being buried in any addiction causes one to make blind decisions that ultimately need to be accounted for. It is only in the bright light of awareness that the ramifications become apparent. The courageous one will weather the tumultuous effects of his unconscious decisions knowing that, in time, after he has taken responsibility for those decisions, stillness will again emerge.

Karma is like puddles of energy spilled in the past, remaining in the present, and often overflowing into the future. To eliminate karma is to clean up the puddles—to claim them and then to deal with them, and then to make decisions in the here and now based on what will support the flow of life rather than constrict it. Once excessive karma is cleaned up, inner guidance becomes loud and clear. Whether that guidance comes in the form of inner peace or an audible voice, it gives detailed information about what needs to happen moment by moment to honor the expression of our essential self.

Repairing one's container includes taking stock of existing karma followed by consciously taking responsibility for our decisions through our actions. At times, the action that is needed will be internal, such as processing feelings of remorse or sadness. Other times, a physical action will be necessary. One might contact a long lost sister or apologize to a neighbor. Cleaning up karmic spills has only one universal law: that we be conscious and in alignment with our higher selves. The life essence that lives at the core of our being would always have us act with love in the present moment. If we do not learn to honor life in the present, we will have an opportunity to try again. This is the essence of karma.

Beyond Back and Forth

There is a period of time on the path to ascension during which we may go back and forth between authentic self-expression and environmental consumption. A day or two of a healthy routine may be followed by an unaffordable shopping spree. Or perhaps a week of healthy eating is followed by a fast food binge that leaves one feeling bloated and greasy. If the addiction is extremely toxic such as drug or alcohol abuse, the behavior needs to be stopped. If not, cherished relationships weaken and break, and the physical body experiences the same.

Aside from obviously harmful addictions, there is a huge gray area that encompasses seemingly innocent behaviors performed in an addictive manner. There is an unlimited number of behaviors that fall into this category—in fact, most any behavior performed unconsciously or obsessively may become addictive. For this reason, while it is necessary to eliminate the addiction, eliminating the behavior entirely may be unrealistic.

Let's look at an example. Jake, an adventurous man who divorced more than fifteen years ago, shared his confusion about his need to "go out every weekend." He explained that he finds himself compelled to "hit the town" on Friday nights to engage in the singles scene. The energy, for him, comes from enjoying the exciting nightlife, having a few drinks, and talking to women. He added, however, that more often than not he wakes up depressed the next day, and it takes him several days to find his center again after a night out. During mid-week, in between recovering from his night out and preparing for the next, Jake's energy is flowing from within and he feels like "himself." If he were to resist the temptation to go out several weekends in a row, the addictive, short-term energy jolt would be replaced by a more consistent (and fulfilling) flow of authentic self-expression.

More and more people are tired of alternating between authentic self-expression and worldly consumption. Would it be practical for Jake never to go out again? Not likely. The ultimate change that is needed is a shift in inner orientation. Jake may decide that he no longer wants to go out every weekend, although he would like to attend special events as they arise.

To avoid the drop in energy that proceeds any consumptive binge, an *expressive orientation* must be adopted while engaging in the previously unconscious behavior. Adopting an expressive orientation means that you maintain a calm awareness while consuming. It is impossible to consume like an addicted wild animal while maintaining a state of calm awareness. In truth, as we go through our day in a state of awareness we are allowing energy to move through us, which is our real source of nourishment. Addictive behavior actually blocks this flow in order to snatch energy from the outside in. In addition, it takes more energy to recover from the addictive action than is initially consumed. We may borrow it, getting an immediate short-term boost in our system. However, because it is borrowed, it is not deeply integrated, which explains why a drop in energy always follows the initial rush.

The answer to eliminating non-harmful or mildly harmful addictive consumption is to focus on one's state of mind and motivation, rather than trying to eliminate the activity altogether. If we simply stop engaging in the gray area behavior, without awareness of the motivation behind it, it is likely that another addictive activity will replace the original one. How does one stay centered while approaching an activity that has previously been a source of immediate external energy? As is true whenever we are trying to break a pattern, being aware of the illusory promise of "getting something" is the first step. The second step is choosing to stay grounded within oneself while engaging in *any* activity. This means to keep one's energy in the body rather than allowing it to jump out and attach itself to the object or activity of choice. Keeping energy centered in our deeper self and in our body is achieved through conscious intention to do so and by remaining aware of the deeper source of spiritual energy present within each breath. With time this simple shift in inner orientation allows one to take part in previously compulsive activities with moderation and grace. Therein lies the key to maintaining an expressive orientation–we continue to rest in and express our essential self, transforming previously compulsive consumption into conscious communion.

Relationship Dynamics

LET'S FACE IT. The question of who holds the power is one of the trickiest aspects of any relationship. There are "power struggles," "power plays," "power trips," "control issues,"–I could go on and on. Although we continuously attempt to manage the power in our relationships, there is usually little discussion about what is actually happening.

For example, John says to Karen, "I will be home at 5:00." 6:30 rolls around and there is no sign of John.

Karen calls his cell phone and it goes straight into voice mail. Her energy is streaming toward him as she waits angrily until he walks in the door. Upon entering the room John hears, "Where have you been? I've been worried sick! How dare you make me wait like this without calling!" She attempts to recapture some of the energy that has been pouring out during the past hour and a half.

John, feeling attacked (because his energy was snatched unexpectedly), retorts, "WAIT A MINUTE! My meeting ran over and my cell phone was dead. You need to back off!"

They go back and forth until each is exhausted. You might think the argument is about being late, and on the surface it is. But the real struggle is one of power.

Power and energy are related. Power is the result of receiving energy. This is true whether the energy source is external or internal. When the source of power is internal, the person has a sense of purpose and direction that cannot be shaken by environmental instability. When the source of energy is external, whether it comes from the adoration of other people or from the superficial status that monetary wealth provides, the resulting power is precariously fragile. Take away the money or adoration and the power it provided is gone as well.

The fact is that, despite its fragility, people often are lured into the false promises of external power. Once we understand that true power comes from within, we naturally begin the process of realigning ourselves with our internal source of energy. All too often, however, this shift occurs very late in life when competing for external energy is no longer a desirable option. One of the goals of this book is to expose the pervasive myth that an external accumulation of energy can provide happiness. Once that myth is shattered we can begin to focus on the real source of fulfillment and inspiration that is often discovered only by wise old men and women. One of the primary areas where energy exchange is misunderstood is energy exchange in relationships. Let's take a look at how this occurs in the many scenarios that are played out as we mistakenly look to our relationships as a source of external energy.

Anyone who has ever fallen in love knows that the surge of energy felt in the beginning of a relationship is enormous. This is one explanation for why new lovers look and feel high, as if "on cloud nine." Those who remain in a relationship for a long period of time know that this intense exchange of energy begins to change form as the relationship matures. After several months or years, it typically shifts into either a mode of stagnation or a mode of growth. Either the couple falls into a routine characterized by a set of ongoing power struggles, or they consciously and continuously choose to work through their challenges to attain a level of mutual respect and a balance of power. Frequently, couples who fall into the former category do not understand that these ongoing struggles are an attempt by each person to gain energy and power. Couples who choose the relationship as a forum for growth tend to be aware that energy primarily comes from within, and understand the fruitlessness of seeking it elsewhere.

Power struggles within a relationship are an opportunity to identify each member's personal strategy for obtaining energy. During the all too familiar tension of a power struggle, no one wants to think about the opportunities for learning about oneself. In fact, it may seem that just to get out of the struggle alive or without permanent damage would be a major achievement. Once the immediate struggle is over it is valuable to examine each partner's expectations and evaluate whether or not it is the other person's responsibility to fulfill them. Often, both individuals are seeking something that can only be supplied from within.

It is important to remember that, regardless of the ways that we attempt to capture energy from our partner, what we are really searching for is self. Real, pure, fulfilling energy only comes from within. Clearly, we have forgotten this essential truth while in the trance of our external pursuits. Our relationships can contain addictive dynamics that are no different than other external energy sources. Just like a stiff drink can give us a temporary high, we can get a different kind of energy boost from another person. Some of this is natural and healthy. We do exchange energy with people as we relate to them. The problem arises when we become dependent on another for those boosts. Then the all too familiar drama takes over, because relating in a healthy way may not provide us with the extra energy we crave.

Most of the time relationship drama is an unconscious process that occurs when we experience internal dissatisfaction in the presence of our partner. Think of a time when you felt inner turmoil over something that occurred in your day. Perhaps it was car trouble or an unpleasant encounter with a co-worker. When you got home you may not have been thinking of the specific incident that occurred to create an off-balance feeling inside, but if your partner happened to look at you with anything less than total affection–whew, watch out! It is easy to snap at a loved one when we are not connected to our source of energy and inner peace. Once we become aware of what is happening, an internal dialogue can begin. We then say to ourselves (and hopefully our partner,) "I had a stressful day today. I need a few minutes to regroup." At this point it is easy to take a few deep breaths, which is often enough to release the free-floating stress that was just waiting to cause trouble.

It is also useful to reframe any stressful incidents that occurred. That is, to try to look at them from a different perspective. Often this new perspective can help us understand the situation better, and release any negative energy we're carrying from it. For example, if a person cuts you off while you are driving, initially it may be easy to assume that the person is a terrible driver and to allow your frustration to escalate. This negative energy can be released by simply looking at the behavior from a different perspective. Perhaps the person is not a terrible driver, but simply preoccupied due to worries of her own.

Reframing is a powerful technique that can work after the fact as well. The other day I took my daughter Anna to a local butterfly exhibit. She had just turned four and this was a big deal. My daughter and I love butterflies. We always talk about them, and we even have pictures of them in our home. For me they have been a personal metaphor that has helped me get through a difficult transition in my life. Suffice it to say, this was to be a sacred experience for both of us.

As we arrived at the exhibit we were given instructions not to touch the flowers or the fruit, because the oils on our skin could harm the butterflies. We entered a large tent, and the feeling was just as I expected. There were beautiful plants everywhere, mist floating down from the ceiling–and yes, butterflies of every shape, size, and color fluttering all around us.

About ten minutes into the experience my daughter placed her hand close to a flower in hopes that a butterfly would land on her. A woman came up to us and very sternly scolded my daughter for potentially "killing the butterflies." I became angry that someone would be so stern with a toddler. I expressed my feelings to this woman, even though it left a terrible uneasiness in the pit of my stomach. So much for our sacred experience with the butterflies!

As we left the exhibit my daughter asked me, "Mommy why was that lady so mean?" It helped me to release the uneasiness by explaining that the woman loved the butterflies and did not want them to get hurt in any way. I went on to explain that people sometimes make mistakes, and that she likely did not mean us any harm. This explanation put the experience in a more compassionate frame, for me as well as my daughter. As a result I found it easier to let go of the frustration I had been carrying.

Emotional Management

WHEN DRAMA OR SEEMINGLY IRRATIONAL EMOTIONS present themselves in a relationship we have the opportunity to look at how we are attempting to gain energy from another. Drama often looks like an emotional struggle over who has control. Later we will look where the need for control comes from. For now it is enough to say that the need to control another is simply a distraction from oneself. Often it is easier to attempt to control our outer world than look within for the source of discontent. The reason we prefer to look elsewhere is because it seems easier. That couldn't be further from the truth. Trying to control the environment rather than dealing with our own feelings is like trying to get the clouds to stop raining instead of choosing to go back inside the house to keep from getting wet. We can be very thick about this—we keep trying and trying despite the fact that it doesn't work!

We can begin to approach things in a more conscious way through emotional management. There are two aspects to this process. The first has to do with the practical aspects of dealing with others in a way that allows them to learn their own lessons while we take full responsibility for ourselves. The second is the intense and often uncomfortable feeling that comes from going within when emotions are high.

Let's take a look at the practical part first. In reality, it is up to you to define limits regarding how others may treat you. If your partner is treating you in an unacceptable manner, it is your responsibility to address it and to take it seriously. If the unacceptable behavior continues after you have shared your position, then you must choose between accepting that behavior after all, or providing some sort of a consequence. Sometimes stating what you need is not enough, and further action is required. If your partner is doing something over and over that is not tolerable it is because you have allowed it.

I am a big believer in boundaries. That means figuring out what is important and living by that. Therefore, step one is defining your values. What is important to you? Is it a wholesome lifestyle, financial responsibility, emotional intimacy, a clean house? For all of us there are things that are crucial and things that are not. For me, a clean house is not worth fussing over, but emotional integrity is a priority in relationships with people I care about. Therefore, I am not willing or able to be in a relationship where feelings are not expressed and honored.

One of the major difficulties with developing healthy boundaries in relationships is that we often put the cart before the horse. We fall in love and then do everything we can to make the relationship fit into our value system. So you fall in love with prince or princess charming and then realize he drinks a bit too much (or maybe a lot too much), or that he works 15 hours every day. What do you do? Each time the behavior becomes offensive you can get angry and explode, which more often than not doesn't work. Another approach might be to know what you value in advance, and then take a new relationship slowly so that when unacceptable behavior comes up you can address it early on, when the stakes are not so high. You may even decide it makes sense to let go of the relationship before it becomes too serious.

There are times, however, when something comes after the relationship is well established. The same rules apply–we have to state our feelings and limits right away and, if they are not honored, we have to be prepared to act. This may sound harsh, but what is really harsh is when people have the same fights over and over with no resolution. When one person is unsatisfied she may feel like she is beating her head against the wall, while the other person feels like he is being controlled. The whole system results in both parties avoiding the ultimate task of personal responsibility.

The solution lies in taking a firm stand against chronic, unproductive power struggles. Step back, observe what is happening, and decide what is acceptable and what is not. You may realize that some of what you have been arguing about is nonsense, and that it is appropriate to simply let it go. Other times something serious might be happening that makes finding inner peace impossible.

A woman named Alice came to see me about her crying spells at work. During our first meeting she confided, "I do not have a good marriage." She also shared that she was a breast cancer survivor. Later I learned that for nearly thirty years she had been living in a marriage where there was no emotional connection at all. Intuitively she felt that it was killing her. It was time to make a stand or potentially lose everything–even her life. Alice told her husband that she could no longer live like that and asked that he work with her to makes some changes. Things changed slightly for a couple of weeks, and then he told her that "it isn't working." Alice and her husband ultimately decided to end the marriage.

I still see Alice, and each week she comes into my office radiating more and more life energy. I now see joy in her eyes and hear hope in her voice. She told me that making the decision to take a stand in her marriage was more difficult than going through treatment for breast cancer. It was the biggest risk of her life, but ultimately she found that it gave her back her life.

Leaving a relationship is not the right answer for everybody. But being willing and able to leave is often necessary for major changes to occur. Pain is a signal that we need to pay attention and possibly take action. The cost of ignoring it is too high. We are living in a time when everything about relationships is changing. It is important that we take responsibility for our own happiness, because in doing so we are teaching others around us that it is okay for them to choose happiness as well.

I believe that, as a species, at this time in our evolutionary process we are on an accelerated path to emotional self-sufficiency. I believe we are being called to heal our vessels so that we are better able contain and express emotion. Why? Because emotion is energy in motion. It is feelings attached to spirit, and is meant to flow freely through our bodies. Yes, it is intense. Yes, it is all consuming–and all transforming, as well! It keeps us flexible and young and humble and in our proper place, which is totally out of control. Life is in control, even when we deny that it's true. Life will always be in control. We have two choices: We can learn how to support life energy, or emotion by allowing it to pass through us, or we can resist it and get physically or emotionally sick. The way we resist it is by excessively focusing on the outer world or on others' behavior. We support it through to process of building emotional self-sufficiency. Emotional self-sufficiency is different than being emotionally unavailable or vacant. It is being able to experience one's feelings without the need to manipulate another to fill the holes from past wounds.

How do we become emotionally self-sufficient? We step out of denial and into what is really occurring around us. We observe, we feel, we allow for what's real. Sometimes what is real is that we are not being valued. Sometimes we find that we are contributing to an emotionally toxic environment. We need to take responsibility for creating an environment that promotes our own inner peace. We learn to live by our values–with integrity. And in doing so the people around us are brought to a higher level of existence. Those who are not ready need to be allowed to live according to their own standards. We need to release them and trust that they will do what is best for them. This may mean making radical changes in our relationships. It is a difficult process. Most often everyone goes through pain and grief when the form of a relationship changes, even though it is often the most responsible action to take when a deep need is not being met.

Carrying the emotional weight of a person who is not ready to be personally responsible is a form of enabling, or helping them to stay at that level. Enabling serves no one. When we enable another person's negative patterns, we pour our energy into that person. It is a form of subtle control on the part of the enabler, but it actually keeps both people from growing. The unconscious goal in enabling is to keep the person dependent upon us. Both people end up being dependent upon each other. The enabler needs to be in control and the person being artificially helped (enabled) begins to depend on the support. Therefore, the person acting as an enabler avoids his or her own work, and the person being enabled is denied the opportunity to feel the natural consequences of their actions.

That is the practical part. It is the reality of creating boundaries in a relationship. The part that we don't often talk about is how desperate the whole process can feel. It can be viewed as a form of "mini-death" in that we are letting go the part of our ego that is trying to control life. Death always feels terrifying at a cellular level. However, though it may feel like death, the process can more accurately be described as transformation. We are living in a time that calls us to transform over and over again. We might as well get used to it: pain, terror, going into the unknown, and then emerging as a butterfly! That is the process. Unfortunately, as difficult as they are, none of the stages of true transformation can be bypassed.

Because transformation, or mini-death, is such a frightening process we may choose to avoid it for a very long time. I remember when I was getting ready to deliver my baby girl and my water broke. As soon as I realized what had happened I became terrified–literally frozen with fear. I crawled into my husband's arms and just cried. I didn't want to move for fear of what was to come. The only way I can explain it is that it felt as though my cells were in fear for their lives. I was experiencing a primal fear of death. I know it doesn't make sense, but that is what transformation feels like. I have felt it since in conjunction with other major life changes. One of the reasons the childbirth example is so poignant is because when we enter any transformation, a form of rebirth takes place. Energy literally changes form and moves through us to be released. This process takes over, leaving no alternative but to surrender. It can cause us to freeze, try to control others' behavior, or drink or eat ourselves into oblivion. Any number of escapist activities may seem like a better alternative than allowing our own spirit to transform us. However, once we allow ourselves to fully go through the terrifying process, we will never be the same.

It may be helpful to look at some of the radiant people you know. You can actually see when someone has surrendered to life. They look full of life. They are beautiful by virtue of their radiance. They sparkle. We want to be around them in the hopes that some of it will rub off on us! They are our role models and once we surrender to our spirit, we become inspirational to others as well.

The techniques that will help you create emotional self-sufficiency are the same ones you learned to help integrate your projections. First, stay with the intense feelings even though they create tension in your body. As we have already discussed, it is important to share your experience with people you trust, though it is best to give yourself the time to burn off some of the emotional residue before talking about it. The temptation to act out on the feeling is too great if we try to talk about it when the emotion is initially triggered or activated. If something comes up that isn't causing intense emotional feelings, by all means talk about it. However, if the feelings are very intense, it's likely that old issues are being triggered, and may need some time to transform themselves. We don't need to do a thing to aid this process except to allow it to happen. Often we can support the process by spending some time alone. We should be aware that picking up a book or turning on the television diverts our energy, keeping it from being present enough to dissolve our emotional blocks so that you can build a stronger vessel for self-expression.

Conflict

JUNGIAN PSYCHOLOGY STATES THAT THROUGH the process of individuation (becoming whole) each of us is headed toward integration as a natural part of life. However natural the process is, becoming a whole individual within a relationship does not happen without some tension. The process of growth within the framework of a relationship requires immense vision and maturity. Growing pains bring with them some conflict. Without an understanding of the process, conflict is often viewed as unproductive rather than an opportunity for expanded awareness. Growth can happen very fast within the context of a relationship. We are given the opportunity to learn how to stand firm and confident in who we are, without need for validation or approval from another. We take a major step each time we address conflict appropriately and bring it to resolution. Each person in a relationship is a mirror for the other to reflect and flush out unproductive ways in which we undermine our own emotional development. For the process to be successful, both parties must be in a position to take responsibility for working through their own challenges. Commitment to conflict resolution must be cultivated in place of conflict avoidance or escalation. Trying to avoid conflict only prolongs its effects. On the other side of the spectrum, escalating conflict to the point of mean-spirited fighting can cause lasting damage. Both avoidance and escalation are attempts to manipulate energy, which can lead to chronic tension that eats away at the foundation of a relationship. When we approach conflict with compassion around our partner's habits of manipulating emotional energy, we create room for growth. When both partners desire true intimacy and sharing, emotional power struggles can be released, building a foundation of trust and intimacy along with emotional self-sufficiency for each person.

Frequently we react to conflict with blame rather than responsibility. We blame the other person for the problems in the relationship. *Focusing on blame is one way that we avoid our own work.*

Inevitably, when both parties do not accept responsibility for the conflict, the relationship begins to deteriorate. Conflict within a relationship is an opportunity and gift of the spirit to facilitate growth and to assist in the process of shedding outworn behaviors.

This paradigm of healing through conflict resolution cannot be extended to relationships where abuse or destructive addictions are present due to the risk of danger. Also, it is impossible to be present while engaging in compulsive behaviors such as abuse or addiction. Only present moment awareness contains the power necessary to transform relationship conflict into growth. In relatively healthy relationships however, conflict can be a speedy and productive way for both parties to blossom.

Relationship Integrity

OVER TIME, RELATIONSHIPS BUILD A container through which emotional energy is expressed, much like an individual's container. Relationship integrity comes from relating in a way that, piece by piece, builds a strong, yet flexible container. A strong foundation provides support during difficult times and flexibility to adapt to the constant changes that life brings. Every interaction that two people exchange will either build-up or tear down this structure.

Looking at the patterns of energy exchange within a relationship can often provide insight into the current state of integrity. Energy is often exchanged unconsciously in relationships. If one person is chronically giving or taking energy from the other, a sickness, or disruption, in the relationship will eventually emerge. When disruption eventually appears it can come as a bit of a surprise. I think most of us have had the experience of all of a sudden becoming aware of an imbalance. We say things like, "It just hit me," or, "All of a sudden the problem between us became clear." Some relationships have a strong enough base to begin healing at that moment of awareness, while others deteriorate and eventually end.

Continually having an awareness of the energy exchange patterns between you and your partner is the most proactive approach to maintaining a healthy relationship. Patterns of energy exchange can be determined by looking at the behavior dynamics in the relationship. Is one person always trying to draw out the other? Does one person monopolize all of the conversation, pushing the other away? Simply observe the behaviors and then ask yourself in what direction the energy flows. Is it being reciprocated? Observing a dynamic can be very difficult to do. This is true in part because we automatically go into the unconscious dance of the dynamic, and also because our unconscious motive may be to manipulate the energy. The key is to step back and remember to observe rather than manipulate the situation toward a certain outcome. Once you observe the blocks and imbalances, you can begin the work of balancing the system. If an imbalance occurs chronically or over a long period of time, the container of the relationship will become fragile and eventually crack open. This wounded state can provide an opportunity for healing if both parties are willing.

A healthy relationship will be strong enough to contain intense emotions. Just as emotions naturally flow through individuals, they naturally flow in and through relationships. This occurs when each person has the ability to be present while containing and expressing strong and intense emotional energy. Trust and support in the relationship are the other essential ingredients to having the relationship be a strong emotional container.

Often we are drawn together because one person has what another is lacking. The natural growth process will invariably provide opportunities for each party to develop fully within the relationship. Through this maturing process a strong relationship container emerges simultaneously as the individual container is built.

People often hold on to destructive patterns of relating because they are familiar and the unknown can be frightening. The unhealthy energy exchanges can go on for so long that they begin to define the relationship. At this point, people often fear that if the familiar pattern ends there will be nothing left and the relationship itself will end. In this sense the exchanges, despite the fact that they are unhealthy, are viewed as a way to connect or communicate with one another. This form of connection temporarily ends when one of the partners withdraws from the unhealthy dynamic, or stops playing their part in it in an effort to foster growth in the relationship. With perseverance, however, what ultimately follows is a much deeper and more meaningful communication based on a spiritual connection rather than on superficial power struggles.

It takes only one person at any given time to take the relationship to a higher level. When you were a child and decided to stop playing a certain game with your friend, your friend eventually had to quit too, because it was only a game when both of you were playing. In much the same way, once you make the choice to stop playing a disempowering game, your partner will get the message and may follow your lead. There are times, however, when one individual will not be able to change their unhealthy habits of relating. When this happens a decision needs to be made whether or not to stay in the relationship. For the most part, when one person stops manipulating energy within a relationship, it either heals faster or ends faster. The outcome depends partly on the desires of both individuals and partly on the soul or destiny of the relationship. Continuing to "play the game," however, is what causes unhealthy relationships to go on and on without any resolution.

Commitment in a relationship means loving the other person unconditionally. Too often we feel that when a commitment is made it comes with a license that gives permission to mold and change our partner as needed. People grow best in an environment of love, forgiveness and acceptance. The strongest relationships are built when both parties know their limits and set firm boundaries accordingly. We can do this with love and with the intention to take care of ourselves rather than with the intention of changing the other person. To be yourself and allow your partner to be him- or herself with no strings attached is unconditional love. If it turns out that the choice is to end the relationship, that in itself can be an act of unconditional love.

The vision we hold of another person carries energy. A judgmental vision carries with it heavy oppressive energy that can feel imprisoning. A non-judgmental vision provides space so that the other person can move and grow. Over time, the vision of the other person affects the relationship, either in a negative or positive way. We have all known marriages that end in divorce after years and years spent with one another. One person is often saying they need "freedom." I don't believe this freedom is usually based on the desire to go out every night or even to date other people. I believe that most often it refers to a need for space–space to be oneself and to transform, move, and grow. An open, ever-evolving vision is the biggest gift we can give another person. It is also the best guarantee that a relationship will endure.

Taking the time to "fuel" oneself from within is essential for long term relationship success. There are many ways to nourish ourselves as we shift from a dependence on external to internal energy. Nourishing ourselves from within, rather than depending on our partner to feed us, is a daily necessity and is the only way to make interpersonal drama and other addictions obsolete. Only you know what feeds your spirit. I recommend utilizing a variety of approaches depending upon your interests. Everyday activities can work as well as more traditional techniques, such as meditation and writing in a journal. Exercising, painting, gardening and even embarking on a long overdue cleaning project are excellent ways to quiet the mind and center oneself. A constant reliance on internal nourishment creates the space for relationships to be based on sharing interests and giving love rather than energy dependence.

When a couple goes through the fire of transformation by choosing to become conscious of previously unconscious patterns of relating, something wonderful happens. A healthy relationship in which both people find their own source of internal life energy is born. The relationship takes on an interdependent rather than dependent flavor. Learning to rely on oneself for spiritual and emotional validation often coincides with the discovery of one's gifts or individual purpose in life. There is nothing more attractive than two people who are each living their life's purpose TOGETHER. It is not necessary for one person to sacrifice himself or herself for the sake of another. Nor is a deep compromise of one's core values necessary for two people to live their unique calling together. Spirit does not demand deep compromise in which both people give up part of what they want to maintain some misguided sense of fairness–unless you are talking about inconsequential choices such as what restaurant to eat at or something of a similar nature. In fact, spirit does not comprehend compromise because when one person is doing what he or she is called to do, it benefits everyone. We are all one at a spiritual or energetic level. Living, speaking and planning from this place produces collaborative win-win arrangements.

Power Struggles

Early on in life we develop ways of interacting with people in our environment to get our needs met. The universal needs of a child are love and attention. Ideally, love is provided unconditionally along with structure and discipline to help the child develop a strong ego, or container, in early childhood. Sadly, there are many adults who are not able to provide their children with loving support and positive discipline. Rather, our moods, inappropriate beliefs about child rearing, and our own personal issues get in the way of consistent parenting.

When love is conditional upon a child "acting right," the child learns alternative ways of getting the love and attention he needs. Withholding energy or emotional support as a way to punish for "bad" behavior or to train him how to act, is a form of abandonment. Abandonment can also occur when a parent is distracted by an addiction to something or someone. Children have not yet developed their own ego container and are therefore depending on their primary care givers for unconditional support and loving discipline as they learn the delicate balance of self-expression and boundaries. If we are too indulgent with our children, they lack the boundaries and self-discipline necessary to contain their spirit. Just as frequently, parents pull back and withholding affection from their children when feeling angry or overwhelmed. When a parent withdraws emotionally she literally trains the child to act or behave in ways that are manipulative simply to avoid abandonment.

An unresolved fear of abandonment can carry on into adulthood, and is one of the primary reasons that we engage in power struggles in our adult relationships. We literally attempt to capture another's energy so that we won't be abandoned. When as a child a person developed ways to compensate for conditional and intermittent parenting, chances are that as an adult she will be unaware of her pattern of controlling or manipulating her environment. Some people manipulate others for attention and security by acting needy, behaving like a victim, or even being cool and distant so people will ask, "What's wrong?"

If we got a glimpse of two people in such an interaction, we could label it "game playing." However, most of us have our own mode of operation that we employ when things are not going our way. These interactions are learned as a way to manipulate external energy. In a close relationship, as with a partner or family member, these behaviors ultimately lead to power struggles. Eventually we must replace these old coping skills with healthier, more creative forms of self-expression.

In addition to childhood emotional trauma, spiritual crisis may also cause an adult to experience feelings of abandonment. Until a person gets in touch with their essential spiritual nature, they will fear abandonment from loved ones. This is because they believe that energy and the attention they crave come from people and worldly pursuits. Therefore, both an understanding of spiritual reality and a relationship with one's inner self are essential to releasing deeply ingrained patterns of attention-getting or environmental manipulation.

Once we allow ourselves to be fueled from within, we can begin the process of letting go of behavior that creates power struggles within relationships. This new awareness makes it clear what direction we need to take.

It also provides the conviction to do the work it takes to change. Once my spiritual world opened up, I believed my behavior would just fall in line with my new view of reality. This did not happen. Despite the immense power that came from getting in touch with my spiritual nature, it still took (and continues to take) deliberate effort to align my behavior with spiritual reality. And yet, all the effort in the world would not have been enough to set me free without my new-found spiritual base, which provided the conviction to change. Conviction along with consistent and deliberate effort eventually amounts to personal change.

Power struggles are a form of manipulation, which are attempts to get energy from another person against their will. From time to time, the attempts at manipulation may be successful. However, we will always hunger for more because external energy is a facade. It does not provide what we are looking for, just as a drop of water does not satisfy a thirst. Taking energy from another does not satisfy the internal longing for a connection to oneself or to spirit.

In the field of domestic violence there is a phenomenon called the *cycle of violence*. The cycle consists of a period of time in which a relationship goes from a honeymoon phase to a phase of tension building (walking on eggshells), to an explosion. This phenomenon is not exclusive to abusive relationships. I have seen many relationships operate in a cyclical nature with no presence of violence or physical abuse. These cycles vary in their degree of intensity and dysfunction, but all are simply progressive states of energy imbalance. The duration of the cycle can be short, so that the couple goes from lovey dovey to mighty fighty in one day, or it can last for months. Often there is a pattern of unhealthy interaction which causes the energy within a relationship to become off-balance, causing one person to give more (time, energy, or effort for example,) and the other to take more. The result is the need to have a fight in order to restore balance within the relationship. Often it is the woman who slowly gives too much and eventually has to recapture her energy in the form of a fight. If the partners are dependent upon each other for energy, the inevitable result will be chronic imbalance.

Identifying the imbalance and its cause is the key to transcending the cycle of violence. Frequently, this unhealthy dynamic occurs because individuals do not take the appropriate time to refuel themselves from within. This leads to a dependency on external sources, in this case, the partner.

Co-dependency is a word that has become a general catch-all for unhealthy relationships. Specifically, it refers to a pattern in which one partner needs to be taken care of and the other needs to take care of someone. In actuality, it is a result of a mutual energy dependence between the partners. Traditionally, one person is addicted, or dependent upon, a substance and the other is dependent upon being a caretaker for the addict. The caretaker is the co-dependent partner. Whatever the nature of the dependency, both people are being fueled from the dysfunctional exchange of energy.

Often the co-dependent partner is trying to control the addicted partner's behavior, therefore this dynamic is a form of a chronic power struggle without a positive outcome, until one person decides to become emotionally self-sufficient.

Over time, the behaviors we use to obtain energy and attention from others become second nature. In extreme cases the behavior becomes an addiction in itself. The techniques used to stop these behaviors are similar to stopping any other habit or addiction. Inner peace is nearly impossible to attain in a relationship based on dramatic power struggles. As we know, because energy is exchanged, there is never any gain obtained from power struggles or emotional addictions. We fool ourselves in to believing that we have gained only to be disappointed later by the lull that follows every dramatic exchange.

Listed below are some valuable techniques to help relinquish habitual power struggles in a relationship:

1. **Increase awareness** – observe the relationship to see what power struggles occur on a recurrent basis. Keep a journal to document details such as when, why, and how they occur. Also, try to determine your role in the struggle, as they are never one-sided.

2. **Unveil the dynamic** – Share your observations with your partner and discuss them without blame. Either verbally or silently take note each time a power struggle starts.

3. **Personal Commitment** – make a choice to "stop playing" by choosing not to engage in the struggle. You may decide to walk away, or both of you may decide to discuss the issue at a later time.

Any time you feel a temptation to engage in a power struggle, DON'T. Because power struggles are centered on trying to obtain tangible energy, this may trigger feelings similar to withdrawal from a drug. Allow yourself to feel the physical sensations associated with the temptation to engage in the struggle, without giving in to it.

Being Connected

Connection occurs when the energy of two or more people literally joins together. This can occur in silence, although we often use words to facilitate the process. We all know the feeling. You spend time with a friend, for example, and during that time you genuinely want to know how she is doing. In the spirit of your interest your energy reaches out and connects with your friend's energy, which is simultaneously reaching out toward you. When you leave her company, you feel nourished and "connected" to her and to humanity in general. This experience feeds us because it is an acknowledgement of our natural state of connectedness at the most fundamental level of our being.

When we do not acknowledge our natural state of connectedness, we are in pain. Sometimes however, the growth that comes out of staying connected can be painful. Feelings flow freely when we are connected to another and to all levels of ourselves. We experience not only joy, but sadness and anger as well. The unpleasant feelings may cause us to become disconnected or to live unconsciously. In other words, when we experience the pain that often comes in the process of relating we attempt to cut off that connection as a way of eliminating the pain.

Positive and negative feelings are a natural and inevitable aspect of relating to oneself as well as to others, but sometimes it's difficult to see how they arise in our relationship to ourselves. Imagine having a baby and treating him the way we treat ourselves. As long as he is cooing and smiling we engage him, but as soon as he begins to fuss and cry we walk away and distract ourselves. This is what we do to ourselves.

This duality in our hesitation to engage the entire spectrum of feelings has a high price. We are fine with happiness and joy but when sadness or anger starts to bubble up we avoid it, block it, stuff it, eat it, and in general create a huge internal mess. Pain and joy are two sides of the same coin. We often forget that avoiding pain also inhibits our ability to feel joy. We could be so healthy if we learned to allow *all* the feelings to flow without resistance. When we cut off our feelings we also cut off the flow of our energy outward, which then becomes the real source of pain.

Communication

The way we communicate with the world has a lot to do with our emotional health. Let's examine some aspects of communication that affect the flow of energy through the body.

We are always communicating. In fact we cannot *not* communicate. We may choose not to speak, however even our silence sends a message. There are three levels of communication. The first includes our thoughts and feelings, which flow in and around us in the form of energy containing information. This level is where we "pick up a vibe." When you perceive that a person is feeling sad despite the fact that he is wearing a smile, you may be picking up the information subtly from the quality of energy around him. The second level is body language and tone of voice. The third level is the most removed from its source and consists of our words. Being aware of how we communicate on all three levels vastly improves your ability to express yourself and connect with others. Clear communication includes being congruent, direct, and concise. Integrating these three elements into everyday communication is one of the best ways to honor the flow of life, while at the same time maximizing the potency of your message.

Congruence

Congruence occurs when thoughts, feelings, body language, and words match. To be congruent is to be profoundly honest. When a person is congruent, they are clear. Clarity comes from having no internal defenses. Integrity is felt in the presence of an individual who is internally clear. If at work you ask a colleague to assist with a project and she says "Okay," but simultaneously looks away and backs up, she is sending you an incongruent message. The word states that the person would be willing to help, but the body language indicates a lack of interest or a feeling of imposition. It is both the sender and receiver's responsibility to ensure that a message is congruent. In this case, you might try to clarify the message by asking if it is a bad time, or by asking any number of questions that may help your colleague feel comfortable enough to share more information. Attempts to clarify are most successful when they are delivered in a supportive manner so that the other person feels emotionally safe and supported enough to reveal the bigger picture.

When we are internally of free of emotional residue our communication is consistent with what we are truly feeling and the messages we send to others are clear. Our energy always reflects our true feelings. However, this is not always the case with our body language and words. When we are full of emotional residue, or have not yet learned to express ourselves freely and directly, the verbal or non-verbal portion of a message can differ from the content of the energy, leaving the message we send to others diluted and unclear. Society in many ways has taught us to dilute our messages. A mother coaching her child in "proper" communication says, "Don't say that, you'll hurt his feelings." We stammer, "How do I put this," as we search for the right words to tell someone we would rather spend a few hours alone than finish the day at a social outing. When we don't feel safe enough to tell our truth, words can lose their significance; they can become a smoke screen, a defense rather than a means of connecting with one another. Whether it is at work or in our own home, all too often we compromise our souls by speaking half-truths. This not only cuts us off from those with whom we are speaking, but it also cuts us off from our deeper self. This point cannot be overstated: Defensive and partial communication hurts our relationships and ourselves.

Conflict resolution training teaches about Position vs. Interest. Knowing your *position* in a disagreement is easy–it is the outcome you hope to achieve. Your *interest* in a certain outcome is not always as clear. It refers to the reason *why* you hold the position you do, and is based on your subjective experience of the situation. Telling someone what your interest is in a given outcome means telling them more than *what* you want; it means telling them why it is important to you. This approach improves the congruency of your message by helping the other person understand your hopes, dreams, fears and insecurities. Our motivation often lives in these more obscure areas that we sometimes conceal for fear of being ridiculed or judged. Sometimes we forget to share our "why" part of the equation out of mere habit. With practice, stating your interest in why a particular outcome is important to you will help others understand–and ideally, to meet your deeper needs.

Say, for example, you and your spouse disagree about where to enroll your child in school. For you, it is extremely important that he be in a private school. However, every time you state your opinion, you get resistance from your spouse. "I don't know why little Jesse needs to go to a private school. Our public schools are just as good, *and they're free!*"

After days and days of discussion, you finally break down and say "Listen, when I attended a public school, I had a very difficult time reading, which isn't a big deal, except that no one ever noticed! It put me at a real disadvantage when I got older because the classes became harder, and the teachers were too overwhelmed to go back and teach me the basics."

At this point, your spouse nods his head and says, "Oh, so that explains why it's so important to you that Jesse attend a private school."

Sharing the "why" does not guarantee that your position will win out. The major benefit of this type of communication is that it adds compassion to the mix. Once the other person understands the reasons behind your emotional stance, negotiation of a mutually acceptable outcome is much more likely.

It is essential in any healthy relationship that a foundation of trust and respect for each other's different feelings are present. Without these two elements, deep communication and conflict resolution cannot occur, and we end up hiding part of our soul to save it from becoming injured. Not only does hiding parts of ourselves diminish the light we experience and radiate, it also has practical implications in communication. When the more personal part of communication is withheld, we end up judging each other based on assumptions. Judgments result in grudges, hidden agendas and passive aggressive behavior, which ultimately eat away at our core and our relationships. Congruent, full communication takes away unproductive guessing and replaces it with the light of knowledge.

Congruent communication comes from deep inside a person. It is undefended, uncensored, and authentic. Finally the message is clean. When communication has the quality of congruence or honesty, the words come from deep within and carry power that is not present in partial truths spoken from the throat. An honest message is spoken with integrity, from an integrated person. An integrated person is not totally free of negativity and judgment, but is willing to acknowledge that these exist. A clean message is free of the residue that covers a censored message. All parties leave the interaction with feelings of completion and satisfaction, which naturally accompany a clean communication exchange. When we leave a conversation having to sort through the content, we can be sure it was not clean. This goes for messages given as well as received. Therefore, if you speak to someone about a pressing subject and leave the conversation confused either one or both of you probably did not speak cleanly enough. Congruent messages carry clean, powerful energy, and the energy is used efficiently, feeding both parties. "Dirty" messages linger, and have to be cleaned up and deciphered later by both parties. Therefore, unless listeners are extremely diligent, there is a good chance they will not get the mes-message at all.

As we discussed earlier, projections are hidden parts of ourselves that we end up seeing in others, and continue to react to until we accept them as our own. When we are willing and able to look at our own shadows and see all the different parts that live within ourselves, we can take the reactive element out of communication. Every message carries an objective content and a subjective content. The objective content is the part that is fact. Most of the time, both parties can validate the facts involved. The subjective content is how the facts effect us or how they make us feel. If we have strong emotion regarding communication with another person, it is likely that part of what we are facing is our own hidden self. During this type of highly charged encounter, the emotional content is shot back and forth between the parties, while the issue at hand gets lost. I highly recommend exploring your part in these types of loaded interactions. They are loaded because they involve much more than just the facts. Identifying the part of your reaction that is irrational is an excellent first step. It can be explored further by looking at what part of the other person reminds you of yourself, as well as the parts of them that remind you of your early caregivers or other significant people in your life.

John and Samantha had been married for two years, and were having a difficult time when they came in for counseling. Samantha shared that she often felt that John was not communicating with her fully. It turns out that his mother micro-managed him along with his brother and sister when they were growing up. She wanted to know every detail about what was happening in each of the kids' lives, and she wasn't too shy to state her opinion on any subject. In response to his mother's communication style, John had become a very private person. Samantha told me, "I can ask him a benign question, like, 'What are you planning to do after your appointment?' and, depending upon his state of mind at the moment, he can find my question controlling." Although she feels left out and offended, in reality it isn't her question that is causing John to become defensive. He is reliving the dynamic he shared with his mother a thousand times–a hot spot is being triggered and he is projecting it onto Samantha.

For John to learn to be aware of this shortly after the conflict occurs will take some attention and effort. However, once he is able to spot it and communicate it to Samantha, it will have incredible benefits for their relationship, not to mention the healing effect that comes when this sort of insight occurs. Knowing that John's defensiveness is a reflex that he is trying to be more aware of frees Samantha from taking it personally, and allows them to move through the conflict quickly while building their communication skills and the integrity of their relationship.

Too often people choose not to communicate at all. This is because one person's shadows are dancing with the other's shadows, and neither is aware of their own involvement in the difficulty. This unspoken dynamic can keep a relationship in a state of chronic chaos. It is best for everyone involved to willingly get messy by going to the deeper level of a conflict. It is like removing an entire splinter rather than just cutting off the top. Removing it entirely can be a little painful in the beginning, but it keeps the area from getting infected in the long run.

The same is true in relationships. When awareness sheds its light on a previously buried pattern, we gain the ability to separate the emotion of our past struggles from present circumstances. It then becomes easier to manage the intensity of our emotions and communicate more effectively while addressing the situation at hand. Whether or not you choose to share with the other person the part of your past that became triggered depends on the level of trust in the relationship. Simply having a deeper understanding will ultimately free you from the prison of a projection. Messages that you exchange with this level of awareness will be pristine and highly effective. If we are willing to take that extra step in communicating with congruence, we keep the relationship clear and allow love to continue to flow back and forth.

Good Boy, Good Girl

MANY TIMES WE ARE SO STUCK on being "good" that we are afraid to truly reveal ourselves. This fear can result in defensive or dishonest interactions. Picture yourself with shelf dividers in your body. Deep down live your biggest fears, traumas, insecurities about who you really are, and your essence. This is also the place where your power comes from. If you are afraid to look at your fears, a lid is put on them, not only keeping the fears in place but cutting off your powerful life essence as well. Using the container analogy, it becomes impossible to block only the "bad" stuff without paying the enormous price of losing the good stuff as well. That's why it's so important that you become able to express yourself, including both the good and the bad. It is only through this process that you will become integrated and congruent.

Expressing the hidden part of yourself is difficult at first, for two reasons. First, chances are that part has been suppressed for a long time, and when it finally comes out it is likely to explode. It is not natural for the body to store emotion. You are vessels of expression, not meant to store life, but channel it. Because it takes energy to hold on to emotions, this energy acts like a lid on a pressure cooker. When the lid is removed, the contents explode—at first that is, until you give yourself permission to express uncomfortable emotions on an ongoing basis.

The second reason it is difficult to express yourself after years of habitual suppression is lack of practice. This is why it makes sense to simply start you are, even if the words sound ridiculous or crude, and in time diplomacy will begin to develop. After some practice you will learn how to say what you mean in an honest way that does not attack the other person.

Many of us have been exposed to "I" statements at some point, whether advised by a marriage counselor or learned in a class on assertive communication. "I" statements are a tool used in communication that allows a person to state what they are truly feeling without blaming the other person. The reason this tool is so effective is because when we take responsibility for our feelings it is less likely that the other person will become defensive. There is a big difference between saying, "I feel frustrated right now with the way things are going," and "You are so frustrating! Can't you just get it right the first time?" The goal in any interaction is to *keep the lines of communication open*. When we blame another for our feelings, the other person instinctively defends out of a need for self-protection, which stops communicative energy from flowing back and forth. When communication stops flowing, baggage starts accumulating and the relationship deteriorates. One of the best things we can do to improve every area of our lives is to learn how to express ourselves while supporting other people, even if we disagree!

Directness

This brings us to the second element of effective communication, which is to be direct. Being forthcoming in communication does not include being hurtful. Keeping the focus on our own experience and feelings makes it less likely that the other person will be hurt in the process.

Communicating in a direct manner means stating the core of what is happening rather than dancing around it in hopes that the person will somehow get what we mean. It is difficult to state the core feeling and experience of an issue, in part because of our perception that the other person won't be able to handle the information we share. This concern may to rooted in our own fears of rejection and abandonment. We end up pouring a lot of energy into communicating in a way that will keep us in other's good graces, only to deliver a distorted message or, worse yet, one that has no impact. My point is this: The more accurate and soulful a message, the more energy it carries. We see this illustrated in music, in poetry, and in all other excellent art. Sadly, we have somehow lost the same passion in our everyday interactions.

Diplomacy, the art of communicating in an unoffending way without compromising the facts, has in many ways been taken to an extreme. Many times we become so concerned with stating our truth in a diplomatic way that the message loses its meaning all together. So we end up going from one extreme to another, either tiptoeing around the center of a message or becoming confrontational or explosive. When we escalate into an attack or, on the other extreme, choose not to say anything at all, we are doing the biggest disservice to ourselves. The more direct the communication, the more power it contains.

I teach an Interpersonal Communication class at the local college. When we get to the section on direct expression of feelings, the class tends to ask more questions than in any other section. Recently a student asked, "What if I'm unhappy in my relationship?" She went on to say, "I would be more comfortable telling him that I am not over my old boyfriend, then telling him the truth." We played the scenario out using both the truth and the "dance around the subject" excuse. Every person in the class ended up agreeing that it saves heartbreak for both people by speaking the truth. Saying, "I am unhappy in this relationship because…" is not necessarily hurtful or unkind–it is, however, difficult. The truth is difficult because it takes courage. However, courage heals everyone involved, even if the information we present is hard for the other to hear.

The other part of sharing difficult feelings ties into our own level of awareness. Often we do not take the necessary time to determine the core issue in ourselves before reacting. A good example is when Samantha's husband thought her question was controlling until he took the time to really look at it. A sense of clarity and direction comes from getting in touch with what is really happening. It takes a desire to understand and a willingness to look deeply into our own thoughts and feelings to discover what we need in a given situation. The clarity that comes from taking the time to understand oneself is the foundation of direct communication. It also puts us in a position to really hear *and understand* the other person.

Concise

Being concise, or "to the point," also helps us achieve effective communication. Much energy is lost in empty words. Just as a packaged cup cake is full of empty calories and provides little long term nutrition, hollow words carry only the amount energy that it takes to say them. In contrast, words spoken from deep down that are concise and brief carry immense meaning and energy that can stick with a person for a lifetime.

Empty communication can be a defense against intimacy or self-expression. If a person was scolded each time he attempted to express himself as a child, it is likely that genuine self-expression is a threatening proposition. I have witnessed empty chatter occurring in most arenas of life. Gossip and endless conversations about topics of little value keep genuine connection far away. The energy received from these types of interactions is the same type of energy received from all external or superficial sources. When it's all said and done, we leave the conversation feeling worse instead of better.

I am not encouraging people to talk less, simply to speak from the heart. Authentic communication that is direct and concise will ring with the clarity and punch of the energy it carries. These types of clean exchanges maximize the power and energy content of the message for both the sender and the receiver. We all appreciate a person who can say what they mean and mean what they say. It is a gift that deepens the satisfaction in life. To truly communicate is to join with another person at the spirit and soul level. To be this type of communicator takes an extremely strong sense of identity reinforced with the knowledge that we do not need to use communication to defend ourselves against attack from another person. Knowing how to express our true thoughts and feelings in a respectful way removes the need for cumbersome interpersonal defenses.

It is not possible to control the way people respond to us. Even the cleanest message can be ignored or manipulated at times. The focus of all effort needs to be contained within our own sphere of responsibility. The way people react is ultimately their choice. When a message is spoken using the above elements, the only guarantee is that we have done our best with pure intentions. From there we are free to move on without feeling lingering guilt and self-doubt. It takes courage to become more honest (congruent), more to the point (direct) and use only the amount of words it takes to express the message (concise). We become more courageous as a result of seeing how wonderful things can be when we communicate this way. Clean communication becomes an essential part of being true to oneself rather than trying to accommodate the ever-changing scenarios of the outside world. Supporting the flow of our energy is the highest goal to have. Expressing ourselves fully, deeply and clearly is one of the keys to keeping ourselves internally clear of emotional build-up, so that our energy can flow freely.

Listening

How is energy related to listening? Our energy joins with another's energy when the other is truly expressing and we are truly listening. In this joining of energy, creation comes forth, new ideas are born, and healing takes place. This is communication and it should not be mistaken for empty words or apparent listening, which is used as a decoy for keeping oneself hidden.

There are people who have learned to drain energy from those who are willing to lend an ear. We have all experienced the person who goes on and on, only to swipe every last ounce of our valuable energy before the conversation ends. This type of interaction leaves the listener feeling exhausted and is, in my opinion, a form of theft. It is clearly unhealthy, for the listener as well as for the speaker. The energy obtained from this type of exchange is borrowed (or stolen) and therefore short-lived. It needs to be replaced soon after its consumption. It also keeps the consumer separated from his or her own eternal energy supply. Feeding people energy by letting them suck you dry is a form of enabling. It is like giving a drug addict their drug of choice, therefore helping the addict stay dependent. Generally speaking, we serve this type of person if we do not fuel their energy addiction. Some of us have difficulty walking away from this type of conversation. I recommend finding a diplomatic way to leave the situation without being hurtful. Getting zapped and strung out are two other energy dynamics that occur during the communication process. Zapping usually occurs during a passive-aggressive, sarcastic, or aggressive exchange that occurs quickly and abruptly. It results in a sharp drop in your energy supply and leaves you scratching your head trying to figure out why you feel suddenly assaulted. A big piece of our energy has been literally snatched away before we can say, "What just happened?" Often, when we are not aware that the communication process is literally an exchange of energy, we are not able to understand these dynamics. We know it is difficult to be around certain people, but we are not sure why. It serves us best if we can identify what really happened as quickly as possible to prevent a knee jerk reaction, which may unwittingly fuel an even more unhealthy exchange. Learning to identify a psychic assault quickly also helps us protect ourselves in future interactions. The only way to respond to these subtle attacks is to expose the dynamic. Saying something like, "Ouch, that comment was brutal!" addresses the hurtful nature of the comment, without getting involved in responding to the actual content of what was said.

Getting strung out, or drawn in another person's direction, is another way of losing your energy to someone else. Some people make a habit of not returning phone calls, keeping people waiting, and selectively ignoring them, and thereby drain energy from them. This type of person will frequently end a conversation by saying, "Call me," or Let's get together soon…" This is a more subtle form of energy theft than the above techniques, and can easily go unrecognized due to the charm and magnetism generally displayed by this type of thief. This type of personal magnetism is not authentic, however. These people literally get their charge from the streams of energy extending from other people who are often waiting for some kind of reciprocity. It can take some time to understand what is happening if your are caught in this type of energy theft. A person who has learned to thrive on the good will of other people is usually very good at giving attention back only enough times to ensure that their following will not lose interest. When dealing with this slippery, shiny type, it is best to quit the game all together and let them contact you. As long as you maintain the expectation or desire for them to return your call (energy) a stream of your life energy will continue to nourish them instead of you.

The highest form of communication happens when two people share their truth, and each is fueled from their core self in the process of connecting with one another. These interactions leave both parties feeling energized, inspired, and connected to the world around them. When we communicate on this plane, we may still have feelings of anger, fear or unhappiness. The only difference is that we take responsibility for these feelings by looking within to find out where they are coming from, rather than blame another for causing them.

There are many activities that can help you become more and more clear within yourself. Writing in a journal can be a powerful tool. I find that when I journal, my deeper self communicates with the part of me that functions semi-automatically. The writing tells me when I am off track or when I am not meeting one of my needs–such as a need for more solitude or more writing time.

All the techniques used for becoming centered in one's spiritual core also assist us in becoming clear about relationships and interactions with other people. They help us learn things about ourselves, such as how we feel or where we need to set boundaries and limits with other people. They also help us see how energies that are leaking or being blocked can be released or reclaimed. As we learn to manage our energy within ourselves and interpersonally, we are lifted into a higher, more fulfilling state of being. From this place, we can choose to join with another or to retreat if we sense that it is not in our best interest to engage. Either way, our interactions are no longer automatic. They are deliberate, healthy, and guided by pure spiritual energy. Our behavior becomes empowering to the people around us because we are teaching personal energy management by demonstration. These healthy, clean interactions nourish our soul's need for connection while honoring our spirit's need for freedom.

In our fast-paced world it is essential that we create situations and environments that facilitate authentic communication. We can and should allow ourselves to truly connect with other human beings. Each relationship can develop unique rituals that support soul communion. It may be as simple as meeting for coffee on a Saturday morning in a soulful place where real conversation has an opportunity to thrive. For a partner, a daily check-in may occur over dinner or before bed. It is too easy to jump into the chaotic, hurried fast lane only to miss the chance to connect on a regular basis with people who are important. Only when we stop long enough to actually *see* one another do our souls dance in each other's presence, giving and receiving energy equally. When that happens we both light up like the sun, radiating energy and nourishment to each other and the world.

A HIGHER LIFE

Redirecting Energy in Everyday Life

BY LOOKING AT THE WAY our lives are organized, as well as the way we relate to money, time, work, and pleasure, it is possible to see clear examples of one's relationship to energy and how it flows (or does not flow) through the body. What was once perceived as objective aspects of everyday life can now be seen as significant symbolism that represents the inner world–the unseen yet absolutely real source of the external world.

As we begin to function more as life intended, like rivers as opposed to dams, the outer world shifts as life itself flows into the thirsty valleys that make up our surroundings. Many things can assist the process of freeing ourselves and simultaneously nourishing those around us by demonstrating the natural process of life. Dreams that occur while we sleep and while we're awake are significant signposts that provide ongoing insight into our progress and our blocks along this path. While awake, we can pay more attention to the content of our "daydreams" for hints about the needs and desires of our inner self. We can also observe how the outer world shifts and opens up with opportunities as we become servants to the will of life energy rather than to our limited self-interests. Sleeping dreams help us to process emotional blocks that we resist feeling in daily life. They also serve the function of giving us information that we are not normally able to see when we're awake. As we pay attention to that information, we gradually become more intuitive and insightful about how to align with spirit energy while being grounded in our soul.

As we shift to a moment by moment reliance on the internal or eternal world, it helps to be aware of the energy dynamics that are present in the outer world. These dynamics can be seen in a number of different forms, including money, time, work, our intuitive knowing, the refinement of energy and death.

Money

Money is the material symbol of energy. The relationship that we have with money is a reflection of the relationship we have to energy and its resulting personal power. There are those who are constantly pursuing wealth in the surrounding world. They are forever working on closing deals or hustling to stay ahead. For these people the same style of pursuit exemplifies the way they obtain energy. Some addictive energy is obtained from the pursuit of money itself, which may be supplemented with cocktails starting at four p.m. or from other excessively consumptive activities. Others may choose a healthier approach, and obtain money by expressing their creative energy in a field they enjoy such as science or art. Money may result from any successful activity though it is attained more effectively through the magnetic force generated by creative expression than from addictive pursuit.

These two different approaches to obtaining money generate vastly different types of personal power. The first is dependent on the continuation of external success. The second type of personal power is dependent only upon the continuation of self-expression, regardless of any external success.

It is also useful to look at one's attitude towards money in comparison to the presence (or absence) of energy flow within relationships and other life circumstances. Perhaps you think that you consistently get little value for your money. Perhaps you feel that money pours through your hands like sand. How does that relate to the energy in your body? Do you constantly feel drained? Do you feel that the energy you expend at work is unappreciated? What about at home? Is your work taken for granted? Or instead, perhaps when money comes to you, you "store" it, hold on to it, or obsessively save the items you buy with the money. In the same vein, do you hold grudges? Do you value secrecy? Do you carry personal problems as a burden in the pit of your stomach or in the small of your back? Or, are you able to share your experiences with others and receive emotional support?

The way we relate to money and other material things is symbolic of how our energy is received, stored, and expressed. If we wish to alter the flow of money in our lives, we must first change our beliefs about energy, since those beliefs will always be reflected on the material level. Once we integrate the understanding that energy is received from within, transformed through the soul, and expressed creatively based on our individual talents, our relationship to energy, and therefore to money, will be in alignment with the natural flow of life.

Time

Time management is such a frequent topic in training and discussion groups that most of us assume we understand the principles. However, we are just beginning to scratch the surface of understanding the relationship between time and energy. Any activity that is performed unconsciously, depletes rather than increases energy in the body. Conscious activity, on the other hand, fuels the body with clean spiritual energy. There are two elements to any conscious activity. First, the activity is directed by the core self. Second, we are wholly present while performing the activity. When both of these elements are present, performing any task is energizing. At the end of this kind of day, the body feels ready to peacefully wind down and prepare for another day. This is a refreshing alternative to feeling drained and thoroughly wiped out.

Earlier we explored how spiritual energy is both expressed and received simultaneously. This is the case when the higher, spiritual self directs our intentions and activities. When intentions are grounded in worldly or material motives, however, the energy expended comes from personal reserves and from the outside environment. Action stemming exclusively from material motivation also sets the stage for a delayed reaction, also known as karma. Energy expenditure is simultaneously replenished only when it is expressed from the core self, which is by nature aligned with spiritual truth. Aligned expression leaves no residue or energy imbalance and, therefore, it does not create karma. All other levels of interaction are simply an exchange of environmental energy. Because it is exchanged, it gives the illusion that one is receiving energy from the interaction.

Consider, for example, gossip, an activity that, when we engage, takes time out of our day. Gossip is a habit that relies on external energy for its survival. It is not a conscious activity because it is driven by the ego, for the ego to get strength. You will notice that when you are in alignment with your higher self, gossip literally brings you down. It lowers your energy to a denser, slower vibration. When one gossips with another person, a sort of exhilarated energy is present. Both parties are actively talking and listening and energy seems to be buzzing between the words. However, the energy is finite, transient, environmental energy. Afterwards, if the individuals are aware of different feeling states in the body, they will feel a certain heaviness. This, again, can only be relieved by another rush of world energy. So, you can call someone or eat a candy bar and get another rush, but after a while the lull in energy always comes back, and you need another "fix" to feel alive. Remember, exchanged energy is only borrowed; eventually, it needs to be paid back. At the end of a day spent this way, don't be surprised if you feel totally worn out.

Chances are you have exchanged a lot of energy, but have not expressed your higher self. Gossip is only one example of unconscious behavior that is draining. Any activity performed with an intention to snatch some short-term energy will have the same effect.

To become energetically in tune enough to be aligned with your core self takes practice, and is difficult to maintain all of the time. Therefore, it is always a good idea to rejuvenate yourself on a daily basis by taking time to do the things that connect you to your core self. Until you are able to live each moment consciously aware and directed by our core self, some depletion will always occur. The more time you spend in conscious alignment, the more energy you will receive simultaneously with self-expression. I have read that spiritual masters need very little sleep. This makes perfect sense when one realizes that they are in a highly conscious state most of their waking hours.

We need to take our approach to time management to another level and conceptualize it as a vertical process rather than horizontal–strive for quality rather than quantity. We have begun to realize it is essential to work "smarter not harder." However, we have not fully grasped what it means to do this. Vertical time management is more fluid than traditional time management because it calls for a moment by moment check-in with the inner self. Have you ever found yourself reading the same chapter over and over again remembering nothing of what you read? When we have moments like this, we are being urged to do something else! Traditional time management would have us follow our list and check off the completed items until everything has been accomplished. When intuition and inner guidance become a part of time management, the rules change entirely. The operating principle is this: If a task is not supporting us in receiving or expressing core energy, it needs to be released and replaced with something else. Alternatively, when our actions are aligned with the core self they will likely be accomplishing many tasks simultaneously. This simultaneous accomplishment is possible because we are working at the level where all life is connected. By addressing the quality aspect of time management in addition to quantity, we increase our energy and improve the level of true productivity that comes from living a conscious life. We bring the timeless dimension (present moment) into time. One woman discovered that if she does what she wants to do each moment, things come together miraculously saving her lots of time. Rather than work on accounting in her home office, she became inspired to go trim a tree in her front yard. Just as she got out the clippers, a man in a truck drove by and offered to do the task for a price that beat all the tree trimming quotes she had obtained the week before. When we allow intuition into the normally linear task of time-management we bring quality, productivity, joy, and synchronicity into our schedule.

This way of thinking differs significantly from the traditional "work during the week and have fun on the weekend" paradigm. Conscious time management is about a different, deeper type of fulfillment than "planned" fun. It is about the joy and inner peace that emerges when we are doing what feels right on every level of our being. The idea of shifting to a holistic, inspired lifestyle can evoke fear, simply because it calls for surrendering control to the part of oneself that lives outside the boundaries of time. We tend to have a hard time giving up control because we are uncertain that the rewards will be as satiating as the blasts of environmental energy that punctuate an otherwise drab existence. The ultimate paradox is that surrendering to the will of life is not about giving up control; it is about taking back control. When we defer daily decisions to the higher self, the only thing we give up is the numbness that accompanies unconscious living. We replace robotic thinking with real or conscious thinking. When our higher self is allowed to function as the leader in day-to-day and moment-by-moment decisions, the very essence of conscious time-energy management is present.

Work

Collectively, we are just beginning to grasp the impact that an unfulfilling job has on an individual. At a societal level, momentum is building toward creating another value system that supports the pursuits of the heart rather than the pursuit of money or security. At an individual level, that shift often involves becoming self-employed or changing careers. The choice of traditional employment versus self-employment is not as important as doing "our life's work," work that is meaningful on a daily basis.

When making a change toward more meaningful work, there is always a risk involved. Some people are afraid of losing financial security, while others wonder if they are being impractical by choosing their dream job. People who do not honor the call of their higher self in choosing a career eventually become hollow shells that perform their jobs with no enthusiasm. Corporations traditionally carried these passionless employees until they retired. However, restructuring and layoffs are now common, as companies look for quicker methods of skimming excess weight off expenses. Losing a job after many years of dedication can be devastating. Although after the period of adjustment, some people find that the life had drained out of their jobs a long time ago. At this point comes an opportunity to find more passionate employment.

When we spend time in a profession that does not utilize our creative gifts, the flow of energy slows to a life-numbing pace. When an individual does not express himself truly from his core, he does not receive energy at a fast enough pace to feel *alive,* and may feel almost as though he is dying a slow death. He may turn to alcoholism, sex addiction, food addiction, caffeine addiction, or a TV or Internet addiction. The direct result of not receiving and expressing core energy is an unhealthy reliance on environmental energy to trick oneself into feeling alive.

There are many books published to assist people in finding ways to make a living that utilizes their natural talents and personality. Many people have found it to be well worth the loss of income or security to make a change that supports their soul. This loss is only temporary, because life supports individuals who support life. By doing what is fascinating on a daily basis, we literally and intensely express more life, energy, spirit, and are lifted into another realm of existence.

Intuitive Knowing

Each unhealed memory carries a piece of our energy. Each obsession, worry, and wound pulls essential life energy away from the body, which dilutes our ability to focus. Pulling back, integrating, and finally transmuting each of these energy fragments allows the formerly extended ribbons of consciousness to wrap themselves back around ourselves and bring the life back into our being. When we pull our energy back into the present and into the body, we are naturally able to see, hear, feel, and sense reality. This heightened perception results in what we call intuitive knowing.

Intuitive knowing is the increased ability to sense the information imbedded in energy. As we are able to hold more energy in our body container, our perception becomes concentrated and information is simply revealed to us through our concrete and subtle senses. The ability to sense the energy conditions in our own body helps us to read energy in the environment. Therefore, the discomfort that comes with the process of reintegrating our own wounds ends in the gift of increased perception of the world around us. This perception can only come when we are able to look without judgment, because when any judgment (or preconceived ideas) are present, pure perception is blocked.

In addition to cultivating non-judgment as a state of mind, we must become emotionally self-sufficient. This means that we are able to handle any feelings that result from seeing the truth. In fact, the level of intuitive ability that is available to us is directly proportionate to the extent that we are able to experience our feelings and accept the truth. Think, for example, of a time when you felt particularly vulnerable. Perhaps it was during a fragile point in a relationship or after you experienced a significant loss. Did you really want to see and know everything? Or, if something threatened to hurt your feelings, would you rather not have known about it? Several years ago a friend of mine went through a break-up that had an element of betrayal to it. She was so devastated by the implications of her boyfriend choosing another woman that she was not able to see reality, much less get intuitive confirmation of the truth. Instead she asked him to tell her over and over that he really loved her and did not want this other woman, which he did–he provided all the reassurance my friend needed to keep her hanging on to the relationship. This traumatic drama lasted for a year and ended up hurting her deeply. When, in the end, her boyfriend married the other woman. When we are not strong enough to integrate the truth of a situation we deny it, cutting off any intuitive information that is available to us.

If we have a lot of emotional congestion that has not been cleared, there is no possible way to see beyond the surface of events. When we are holding on to emotional residue or congestion, we project it onto everything we see and experience in the external world. Our judgments are clouded. Only through the day-to-day work of emotional clearing will we achieve enough stillness and strength to receive intuitive information.

Clear perception, and the ability to reflect that perception back onto another person, is a natural result when we do our own clearing work. Pulling back projections and purifying our energy results in transparency (lack of congestion). When we are transparent, our projections no longer intertwine with another's projections in the dance of drama. Instead, we are able to see the other person clearly without the interference of our own projections. This clear vision includes seeing a person's essence as well as the areas in which they need healing. If we are clear within ourselves, we are able to reflect back the person's radiance as well as their blocks. In many cases it may be the first time that person has had the gift of seeing his or her true reflection. This experience alone is healing because it causes one to shift personal identification from the limited and wounded self to the deeper and eternally healthy self. There is no greater inspiration to heal ourselves than when we catch a glimpse of our totally perfect essence. Transparent people (those who are connected to their essence and devoid of emotional congestion) are healers simply by virtue of their presence. The world is calling for us to become transparent as soon as possible. When we do, we can help the world become centered on love rather than on chaos and confusion.

Increasing our intuitive ability is simply a part of the process. It is not an end in itself, nor is it a tool to be used in any capacity other than as compassionate vision and intuitive guidance. The only difference between individuals who have this quality and those who do not have it is the level of integration and alignment attained, or in simpler terms, the amount of personal energy they have available to live in the present moment. Some people will attain clear vision or intuitive knowing sooner than others, and to keep it they will have to use the gift with integrity. Ultimately, this means helping others learn to see for themselves.

Energy Refinement

Many traditions speak of energy moving up the body as we move toward enlightenment or ascension. Energy becomes lighter as it becomes more refined. Every step of the way, the energy of our being is transformed through our experiences. This process requires nothing more than our willingness to honor a bigger plan, even though it may feel like foreign territory at times. In any case, the goal is not to leave the body and ascend to heaven. It is to live a heavenly existence while we are housed in our sacred body.

During the process of healing, the mind and body work together to incubate and give birth to increasingly refined energy. We can either choose to resist this process as one would resist death itself–by keeping ourselves distracted through addiction or constant life chaos–or we can learn to engage in the ongoing evolution of our mind, body, and soul. The reason many of us unwittingly resist our own enlightenment is because the *feeling* of energy transforming can be one of tension or dissonance. Because we don't talk freely about the process of inner transformation and what it entails, people often just perceive it as discomfort and run the other way.

Engaging this constant transformation calls for a level of trust in the process. Part of the goal of this book is to discuss the process of healing so that it becomes more familiar and less threatening. Until one experiences the uncertainty, discomfort, and eventual elation that accompanies internal energy transformation (refinement), it may remain a very threatening prospect. I have heard people say that as soon as they think they have life figured out, another challenge presents itself. These challenges are simply our natural inclination to evolve or ascend. If we learn to view these unexpected turns for what they are, they will not be nearly as challenging. Once we become proficient in the art of living in uncertainty, the challenges will be more like a bump in the road rather than a mountain in our path. Uncertainty is what defines transformation, like going from black or white to gray. We are uncomfortable with gray because it feels as though we are not in control, and guess what? WE ARE NOT IN CONTROL OF THE ASCENSION PROCESS. Just as caterpillars are not in control of when they become butterflies, we are not in control of when and how we become angels here on earth. Our resistance to engaging this process keeps us stuck individually and collectively. That is why we have become so adept at addiction in all its forms: it is a brilliant way to delay our own destiny.

Part of the ascension process involves embracing rather than rejecting the human body. The mind cannot continue to take more than its fair share of control in daily life. We need to be able to engage in sweaty sex as well as write and recite a romantic poem. The key is to cultivate the inner ability to play all of the notes on the scale of self-expression. To express the highly refined energy of spirit while eating a large meal for our earthly bodies, if we so choose. The difference is a state of inner freedom. We ultimately come to a place where we are not being run by our addictions or worldly ties. When this happens, energy flows through us regardless of the activity we are performing. When we are stuck at a certain level, energy becomes blocked. Everyone becomes stuck at one time or another, but some never do the work it takes to free themselves and rise to another level of potential creation within the body.

When our being is near the next point of evolution we will always experience temptation. This is not temptation as we traditionally relate it to heaven or hell. It is a temptation to return to old patterns, old ways of blocking the flow of energy. Fortunately, this kind of temptation has a very practical function. Its purpose is to clear away any remaining unprocessed energy from the previous level of being.

For example, a friend of mine by the name of Kate told me the story of how she had played the role of a victim in her marriage for twenty-six years. She knew deep within herself that she had more control over her life than she was allowing herself to have. She simply did not know how to change her energy source. After many years of relying on her husband and children to soothe and comfort her in her perceived agony, it was nearly impossible to envision any other way of being. Eventually, her husband chose to leave the relationship because he could not see a way out of his unhappiness. The deep grief and anger that Kate experienced when he left helped her to realize that she had to change her role in relationships. Kate sought the help of a counselor and proceeded to read as many books as she could get her hands on about relationships and emotional health.

When I met Kate three years after her marriage had ended, she had a good job and was feeling very good about the changes she had made, especially in her relationships with her children. She had started dating someone and was ready to start her new life. About six months into the relationship, however, she started to feel that she was being treated unfairly, and mentioned this to her new friend. Fortunately, Kate was able to realize that she was falling into her old patterns once again, and worked extremely hard to rely on her inner self when she began to feel the urge to act as a victim.

Kate is no longer in that relationship—a decision of her own choosing. Rather than allow herself to be mistreated, and to again see herself as a victim, she chose another path. It would have been easy to fall into the same groove that she had with her husband, but this time Kate took the more difficult risk of choosing something different. Now, Kate herself is different. This is an excellent illustration of how once we have attained a certain level of healing, the universe will place a situation in front of us that forces us to choose *again*, so that any remaining part of an energy pattern or addiction can be fully healed.

We will always experience some sort of temptation to return to previous habits. We may even relapse into an old pattern a few times before the healthier behavior takes hold in our psyche. What is important is that we identify it for what it is, a final clearing opportunity, rather than beat ourselves up and think we are incapable of lasting change. As a temptation of an old pattern presents itself and we are able to "walk the talk" of our new awareness, the energy of our being is refined to a higher level.

Death

The topic of death is scary and sacred all at the same time. I am unable to have a discussion in the context of this book that does the topic justice. However, it is so intimately related to the process of managing our energy that I feel compelled to share some brief thoughts on the subject. For those of you who feel inspired to study the process of death further, there are many excellent books that will help you to do so.

At a certain point in time each of us is called to leave this earth. There are many ways to view this transition, and all perspectives are valid. The tragedy comes only when we choose not to examine what it means to pass away from this world.

This book has focused on creating a heavenly existence while we are in our earthly bodies. At the same time, it is a spiritual opportunity to examine and ultimately approach the transition out of the body as an essential and sacred process. All life is eternal. However, when viewed through human perception, we tend to perceive this sacred transition as the ending we call death. Many cultures embrace death with reverence and awe, honoring the process as simply another facet of life. Unfortunately, in the United States and other parts of the world, many of us are paralyzed with fear over the prospect that we may evaporate into nothingness.

It is my feeling that we need to re-examine our beliefs about leaving the body in order to foster a healthier attitude toward the present moment. The process of healing and ascension is not about avoiding or delaying the dying process; it is a process geared toward experiencing the fullness of life. The purpose of doing this work is to be a clear and healthy human being. This worthy goal is accomplished by bringing our currently fragmented energy back into the present moment. We can then begin to live according to the set of rules that govern an eternal, rather than temporal, existence.

The process of transitioning out of the body entails bringing our energy to a point of being that is outside the realm of space and time as we know it. In this process, our energy, which has been spread over a lifetime, is gathering to arrive at the eternal point we refer to as the NOW. As the energy comes together, we start to lose awareness of our environment. We release our attachments to our life here on earth. As this process continues, the immense amount of energy carried in our bodies also begins to detach and culminate into the present moment. When a substantial amount of our life energy has pulled itself into the NOW, it spontaneously ascends and goes back to its source, a bigger pool of energy–the light.

As our attachments are released a final time, we feel the effects of our actions here on earth. Many authors have talked about this instantaneous review of life as we cross over into the spiritual dimension. The quality of energy in each choice we made in life is experienced in full as a final illustration of the golden rule. "Treat others the way we would be treated" takes on another dimension when it is realized that the effects of our decisions are always with us.

The transition process is only uncomfortable in that we are releasing the thoughts and attachments of a lifetime. The brain does not accompany the spirit upon death. Therefore, life has to release itself from the brain just as it leaves the rest of the physical body. This sensation of not being able to maintain lucidity and control of our senses is unfamiliar and can be frightening, though it is a natural effect of life detaching itself from the body. Once the initial discomfort of release is complete, our spiritual self can ascend peacefully.

With this process in mind we can choose to focus on the eternal part (present moment) of daily life through mindfulness and meditation. This is a lovely preparation for the ultimate release. In addition, life presents opportunities continually to practice releasing objects from the grasp of our energy. This process of release is referred to as surrender. Surrender, which allows life to flow where it may, is good practice for ascension here on earth and for our ultimate lesson in letting go when we leave this earth.

Ascension

ASCENSION IS OFTEN ASSOCIATED WITH going away from our body up toward the heavens. It is actually much more natural than that. It is relaxing into oneself completely here and now on this earth. The key is to go deeper into our essence right now–deeper into our feelings, deeper into our fears and deeper into our awareness of our body and mind in the present moment, and the future will take care of itself. When we are clear enough to allow the energy of the present to infuse every cell of our being, we are ascended and living in the realm of heaven and the realm of earth simultaneously. This is a process I refer to as earthly ascension.

Shifting from worldly to spiritual dependence continues as long as one is in this world. Daily challenges still exist, though they become more manageable and more subtle. Problems that do come up are viewed as opportunities to readjust in an effort to be more aligned with spirit. Clarity comes quickly to one who practices inner peace, and clarity brings the freedom to make adjustments with ease. Mother Teresa left us with much wisdom. One of the ideas that she left is that the goal is not perfection; it is consistent intention. As a yoga teacher once told me, every effort provides all of the benefits. The quality of the moment is the source of inner peace, not the amount of experience or time spent on the path.

One of my earliest spiritual memories occurred when I was in my early twenties, during the time that I was obsessed with eating and how much I weighed. I had gone for a walk, though rather than enjoying myself I was obsessively counting the calories I had consumed for the day. In the midst of endless thinking, a calm, peace-filled voice inside me said, "The process *is* the outcome." I spent the next hour walking and contemplating this profound statement, which ultimately provided me so much inner freedom. In that moment I understood completely that I have to choose peace each moment, and that it will not come later–only *now*.

Blessings are an indication that we are following our hearts. One quickly learns that if inner peace, joy, and purpose are not present, then one has momentarily moved off the path. At this point the only appropriate response is self-forgiveness and realignment with spirit.

In the world of manufacturing there is something called a *feedback loop,* which is the mechanism to receive information when a process is off track, and also when it's on track. We all have a built in feedback loop which gives us the same information. From within, we get either a signal of inner turmoil or one of inner peace. Once we get this information, we can use it as an indicator either that we are on the right track or that it is necessary to go within to process unresolved feelings or adjust our thoughts to be in alignment with the flow of life. Just as in the manufacturing world, the ability to minimize the time it takes to make a correction is the key to minimizing time out of production–away from our core.

Realigning with our core self can take anywhere from a few seconds to many months of soul searching once we realize we are off center. While minimizing our time off track is definitely a goal, it is crucial that we do not judge ourselves for the time it does take. Often, the grueling time spent in the gray area of confusion is exactly what is needed in order for clarity to emerge around the difficult issues that each of us must face.

Guilt is one of the biggest obstacles to getting back on track. It masks itself as something virtuous, as if feeling bad becomes a way of repenting. In fact, it keeps us out of spirit's reach only to become submersed in feelings of shame and inner conflict. Forgiveness, or letting go, releases guilt and allows us to hear our inner truth once again. It often takes many tries to shift our focus from consuming energy to aligning with our essence and allowing energy to naturally flow through us.

There are many of us now who are shifting our allegiances from the material to the spiritual world. We are lighthouses for all of our brothers and sisters to find their way. We are in the world, working, socializing, having children, retiring, selling our houses, and buying cars. We are humble in that we know our outer world is simply a reflection of our inner world. Our primary function is to remain focused on keeping our inner world clear for spirit to inhabit. This is the message of *Opening to Life*; it is a way of becoming spiritually whole while living on this earth. And contrary to the belief that one must live in isolation to achieve spiritual enlightenment, living in the midst of chaos in this world is the fastest path to ascension.

Awareness, healing, then ascension. By becoming aware of what shape our container takes, we are able to relax into our natural self as the first step of surrender. Then the work of healing can take place as we confront and release the blocks to expression and repair leaks in our containers. Finally, all the energy that has been previously used to heal ourselves is now funneling through a sturdy, clear container, transforming us at an incredible pace. The spirit that is able to move through clears away any leftover crumbles of unfinished business, preparing to express itself creatively and uniquely based on our innate talents. All the while, our physical containers become lighter and lighter, vibrating faster and faster while simultaneously living a peaceful life and healing others simply by being ourselves.

The physical body and the senses through which we perceive life all change as our state of being changes. Our vision begins to focus on the inherent beauty in all things while viewing the more disturbing aspects of life as the need for alignment. As we work through the inevitable blocks of emotional residue and repair addictive patterns, life is able to simply flow. Thoughts no longer become obsessive or circular; in fact, the purpose of thought shifts entirely to serve the flow of life. Thoughts are often useful in making sense of the raw feelings that we continue to experience. They also serve to bring clarity to the intuitive guidance we receive on a feeling level. Thoughts start to feel lighter and integrated with the body, becoming more like the breath and less like an out of control train. Together each part of our being works in harmony to create a more holistic state of being.

As an overall integration and clearing occurs within the body, the vibration is raised to a higher level cultivating inner stillness. In the stillness, inner guidance or intuition is perceived more readily either through sound or feelings, and it always gives information that serves our higher self. This process then continues to lift us into more refined states of being. The spiritual energy that flows through us is subtle; it feels peaceful, constant, and at times exhilarating. It is immensely freeing and many times more fulfilling to be animated by spirit rather than the manipulated and short-lived high of external energy. With spiritual energy as our source, we cannot determine when a moment of joy will bubble up causing uncontrollable laughter. A welcome, unplanned moment of deep inner peace and total purpose can emerge at the sight of a sunset. These little serendipitous blessings are what come with a life led by spirit, and I do mean *led* by spirit. We are not running the show when our lives are fueled by spiritual energy, and frankly, I am very comforted by this fact. There is not a director in Hollywood who would be able to create the fulfilling and serendipitous scenes that the unseen world of spirit creates. Ultimately, as we become ascended right here on earth. We are used for God's purpose of demonstrating love, compassion, and total well being. We each possess love and life as our core, and the more of us who refuse to allow anything to block our core from shining through, the more we will be able to support each other in building heaven right here on earth.

What a joy to live in a time when so many of us are striving for spiritual integrity. It is becoming an archetypal vein in the consciousness of society. Each day that we embrace our spirit as our self we add to this mounting force that will one day change the world forever.

www.ingramcontent.com/pod-product-compliance
Lightning Source LLC
LaVergne TN
LVHW051557070426
835507LV00021B/2628